CONTENTS

Great Games

RANGERS *v Celtic*

Rangers 5 — Celtic 1, August 1988

Goal no. 4

SOMETIMES we fail to recognise the most significant moments of our lives as they are happening.

The Rangers fans who had been present at Ibrox on the afternoon of 27th August 1988 harboured no such thoughts as they celebrated that Saturday evening. This had indeed been one of their most memorable days — *and they knew it!*

Yet this first Old Firm game of the season had started badly for the Light Blues. Within only five minutes and during a sudden seasonal August downpour, Celtic were one up.

After two attempted clearances by the Rangers defence, the ball fell to Peter Grant whose shot broke to Frank McAvennie from the bottom of Chris Woods' right hand post. The Celtic striker slotted home the rebound. The current league champions were ahead.

With ten minutes on the clock, the 'Gers were level. Ray Wilkins hoisted a free kick into the Celtic box. Butcher, Gough and Drinkell all rose

with the Celtic defence. John Brown pounced on the loose ball at the edge of the area and drilled a fierce right foot volley netbound. Celtic central defender Mick McCarthy's ensuing block fell to Terry Butcher who passed to the unmarked Ally McCoist. 'Super Ally's' superb left foot strike never left the ground as the ball embedded itself in the back of the Celtic net just inside English keeper Ian Andrews' left hand post.

Goal no. 3

Ten minutes before the interval came the goal that will never be forgotten by those thousands who witnessed it that day. A goal that has already become legendary.

A typical long Gary Stevens throw-in from close to the corner flag reached captain Terry Butcher, whose back header was in turn headed clear by Paul McStay. Ray Wilkins was lurking like a predator just outside the penalty area.

To say that his perfectly judged and flighted right foot volley was exquisite, is an understatement. Certainly the Celtic keeper hardly moved as the ball flew past — an exocet missile heading for its target. He could do nothing but spectate . . . and view with grudging admiration!

The noise was deafening. Rangers were ahead and would not be caught. Half time was upon us.

Celtic substitute Derek Whyte appeared at the start of the second 45 minutes in place of Tommy Burns in an effort to stem the tide. But this was a flood tide.

A Gary Stevens free kick was headed clear by Anton Rogan and picked up just outside the box by Ian Durrant. His subsequent cross was back-headed by Ally McCoist towards the Celtic goal. The presence of Kevin Drinkell was just enough as the Celtic keeper badly misjudged and allowed the ball to dip under the crossbar for Rangers' third goal.

The fourth was an absolute gem. Mark Walters picked up a McCoist pass just to the side of the Celtic area, to be faced by Mick McCarthy. The Celtic defender's presence was not enough. A superb Walters cross was met powerfully by the head of Kevin Drinkell. His first Old Firm game, his first Old Firm goal.

The celebrations were led by the inspirational Ray Wilkins. 'Gymnast' Mark Walters showed off his forward roll. Walters and Drinkell embraced. Rangers were 4-1 up and the question now was: "How many?"

An answer was not long in coming. A searching clearance by Chris Woods was headed out by Derek Whyte and intercepted by John Brown, whose first-time ball to McCoist caught Roy Aitken off balance. Ally pounced and headed for goal. Once inside the penalty area, he was illegally brought down by the Celtic captain but before a penalty award could be given, Mark Walters, following up, slotted home the loose ball to take Rangers to five. The rout was complete. A glorious victory was theirs.

Goal no. 5

Supporters lingered outside Ibrox long after the sound of the final whistle that Saturday. It had been a magical day. As the score spread like wildfire throughout the city, many reactions were the same:

"Unbelievable," they said. But it was more than that. It was perfect.

Player Profile

TERRY BUTCHER

When Graeme Souness was preparing his plans for the 1986-87 season, his first in charge at Rangers, two things were high on his agenda. He knew that he needed a top-class central defender and, although Souness would be on the park himself in his role as player-manager, he wanted someone else to take over the job of captain. In Terry Butcher he found the answer to both those problems.

Butcher was playing for Ipswich Town at the time and was already established in the England squad. Several other big clubs were chasing his signature, Spurs and Manchester United among them. Graeme Souness had already been to East Anglia a few weeks before when he signed Chris Woods for £600,000 — a record fee for a goalkeeper — and after a trip to Ibrox to see the stadium for himself, Butcher agreed to sign.

The transfer was announced on 1st August 1986, the fee being £725,000. Looking back with hindsight from a perspective of four years later, it can be fairly said that Souness not only got the man he wanted, he got outstanding value for money. Big Terry has proved a great favourite with the fans both on and off the park and has been an inspiring captain of the club as well as the pivotal figure in its defence.

Terry Butcher had a tough initiation, making his debut for the Light Blues just four days after his signing in a friendly with the powerful Bayern Munich at Ibrox. Rangers lost 2-0 but the Souness influence was already evident, not only in the shape of the team but in the way they played.

In the season that followed, Terry Butcher showed why his manager had been so keen to sign him. His superb timing in defence, his outstanding ability in the air — being 6'4" helps there, of course! — and his readiness to move upfield for set pieces made a major contribution to the new-look Rangers.

The Skol Cup was won in October and although there was a setback when Rangers unexpectedly tumbled out of the Scottish Cup at the hands of Hamilton Accies, they showed excellent consistency in the Premier Division and from February onwards always looked likely to take the title.

The big day came on 2nd May, away to Aberdeen at Pittodrie. A draw was enough, and it was fitting that Terry Butcher should score Rangers' goal with a powerful header. The captain was presented with the trophy at Ibrox the following Saturday.

As so often happens in football, the pendulum swung the other way in the following season. In October 1987 Terry was sent off, along with Chris Woods and Celtic's Frank McAvennie, in an Old Firm game, and a month later he suffered a bad break of his left leg when clashing with Alex McLeish of Aberdeen at Ibrox. The injury would keep him out for the rest of the season.

Terry was back for the start of the 1988-89 season and his partnership with Richard Gough at the heart of the Light Blues defence was fundamental to Rangers' success in landing the Premier Division Championship again that season. With Chris Woods in outstanding form behind them, the 'Gers conceded only 26 goals in 36 league matches.

The success story continued last season, with Terry Butcher leading Rangers to their 40th Championship. He was also a regular in the England team, and few will forget his 'Captain Courageous' night in Stockholm, when he insisted on carrying on in a crucial World Cup qualifier even though he had suffered a bad head cut. By the end of the match, Terry's shirt was covered in blood, but England had gained a vital away point.

Terry is 32 in December 1990 and looks set to stay with Rangers for the rest of his playing career. He is in the great line of Rangers captains that runs from George Young through John Greig, and after four years it is hard to imagine the central defence without his dominant figure.

One last point — Terry is often thought of as one of the most important of Graeme Souness's English signings. He plays for England right enough and he came from an English club — but he was in fact born in Singapore!

Terry scores against Celtic, August 1989

FUN QUIZ PAGE

Rangers in the Skol and Scottish Cups

1. Skol Cup Final 1986. Name the player who won the 'Man of the Match' award.

2. Name the top scorer in the 1989 Skol Cup competition.

3. Rangers won the 1987 Skol Cup Final after a penalty shoot out with Aberdeen. Who scored Rangers' goals in the actual match?

4. Ian Ferguson scored a glorious goal in the 3-2 Skol Cup Final victory over Aberdeen in 1988. Who scored Rangers' other two goals?

5. Rangers' first Skol Cup victory under Graeme Souness was in season 1986/87. Result and scorers for Rangers?

6. Which team defeated Rangers in both the 1984 and 1985 Scottish Cup competitions?

7. Who captained the victorious Rangers team in the Scottish Cup Final of 1981?

8. 1973 Scottish Cup Final. Rangers' opponents and score?

9. Chris Woods' record 'shut out' run in season 1986/87 ended in the Scottish Cup defeat by which team?

10. John Greig's final trophy as captain of Rangers was the Scottish Cup victory of 1978. Who were Rangers' opponents?

Rangers' League Campaigns

1. Who scored Rangers' first goal in the April 1989 Old Firm match at Parkhead?

2. Derek Johnstone entered the record books in September 1975. Why?

3. During above campaign, Rangers lost only once at Ibrox. To which team?

4. Rangers won the League in season 1977/78. True or False?

5. 'Super Ally's' first league goal for Rangers was scored against who in 1983?

6. Rangers scored **seven** goals in a league match season 1987/88. Opponents and goal-scorers, please!

7. Season 1948/49. Who scored three goals against Celtic at Ibrox on New Year's Day?

8. Scorer of the goal that defeated Celtic in the first Old Firm game of 1986/87 season?

9. Graeme Souness' first league goal was against . . . .?

10. Season 1988/89. Scorers of Rangers' goals in the January victory over Celtic?

Answers on page 52

JIM BAXTER

The term 'footballing genius' is overused, but it can be applied with certainty to Jim Baxter. His principal playing career with Rangers spanned only five years, but supporters still talk about 'Slim Jim' with awe and reverence.

Baxter was exceptionally gifted as a player and, like others with extraordinary natural talent, was disinclined to work too hard. He confessed to disliking training and this undoubtedly led to his career ending before its time. He still achieved more than most; he was a bright star which dazzled us in its orbit before the inevitable return to earth.

Jim Baxter started his playing career as a 17-year-old with Raith Rovers in 1957. The Fife club somehow managed to hold on to him for three

seasons before Rangers took him to Ibrox, the fee of £17,500 surely being one of the great steals of all time — in the frenetic international market of 1990 you could probably add another three noughts to that figure.

Baxter was an immediate favourite with the Rangers crowd, not only for his skill on the ball but also for his clowning. He would stand on the ball to taunt opponents, juggle with it and even sit on it sometimes! His arrival coincided with Rangers' first tilt at the European Cup-Winners Cup. They went all the way to the final, but for Jim Baxter and his team-mates it was to be losers' medals, Fiorentina beating the Light Blues in a two-leg contest.

He did, however, get a Championship medal in that first season, and two others in 1963 and 1964. There were three Scottish Cup successes in a row against St Mirren, Celtic and Dundee, and four winners' medals in the League Cup.

Baxter was a glittering star in the international team too, winning 34 caps, one of his greatest moments coming in the 1963 game against England. Scotland won 2-1 and Baxter had an outstanding match, tormenting the English defence and scoring both the Scottish goals.

Season 1964-65 was a less happy one. Baxter broke his ankle in the last minute of a European Cup tie against Rapid Vienna and was sidelined for a good part of the season. In May 1965, to the dismay of the Rangers faithful, Jim Baxter was sold to Sunderland for £72,500.

He would be back: after moving again to Nottingham Forest, he was given a free transfer and Davie White brought him to Ibrox again for the start of the 1969-70 season. There were flashes of the old brilliance but the team as a whole lacked consistency and at the end of the season Jim Baxter left, somehow a sad end to a career that had given all who watched him so many glorious moments.

Football fans will argue endlessly about 'the greatest of them all', and perhaps it is a question that can never be satisfactorily settled. Whenever the debate starts, you can be sure that it will not be long before Jim Baxter's name comes in. Once seen, he was never forgotten, and there are few like that.

It All Came Right In The End

You could summarise the 1989-90 Premier Division campaign by saying that "it all came right in the end." At the end of August 1989, that might have seemed a distant dream. After three league matches, the Light Blues found themselves in the unlikely — and unwanted — situation of propping up the Premier Division with just one point and one goal.

The season had begun with the usual buzz of excitement and anticipation. During the summer there had been the dramatic signing of Maurice Johnston from the French club Nantes, and Trevor Steven's arrival from Everton to join his former clubmate Gary Stevens and add to the growing list of English internationalists at Ibrox.

A pre-season training trip to Italy put the players in fine fettle, and in friendlies before the real action started the team knocked in a dozen goals, Mo Johnston quickly getting his name on the scoresheet against Airdrie, Kilmarnock and his former club Partick Thistle. Trevor Steven also impressed in those early games.

A week before the competitive action got underway, Rangers took on Tottenham Hotspur at Ibrox and came out worthy winners 1-0. It was the ex-Everton partnership that set up the goal, Trevor Steven smacking a thrilling 25-yard shot past Norwegian international keeper Eric Thorstvedt after combining with Gary Stevens. In midfield, Ian Ferguson far outshone Spurs' big money signing Paul Gascoigne.

Premier Division action was set to start on Saturday 12 August with a home game against St Mirren. The day before, manager Graeme Souness said in a press interview: "I know we won't run away with the league title, or even dominate from start to finish, because the Premier Division is too competitive." Prophetic words!

That first match was a shock to the system. St Mirren's well-organised defence repeatedly withstood the Light Blues attack, and the Paisley side scored what was to prove the only goal of the game after 28 matches when Kenny McDowall challenged Chris Woods as the Rangers keeper went for a Dawson cross. The ball ran loose and McDowall slid it into the net.

Woods injured his shoulder in the incident and had to leave the field, Ian Ferguson taking over in goal. This had definitely not been on the pre-match script, but there were many in the 40,000 crowd who thought the goal should have been chalked off for an illegal challenge.

For the rest of the game, St Mirren's Campbell Money was by far the busier keeper. The 'Gers defence protected Ferguson well and he was rarely troubled. Up front it was an afternoon of frustration — no matter how hard they tried, Rangers just couldn't get the ball in the net.

Things went better in midweek as a McCoist hat-trick helped Rangers to an easy 4-0 win over Arbroath in the Skol Cup. Bonny Ginzburg made his debut in goal as Chris Woods' replacement, and stayed between the posts for the second league match, away to Hibernian.

Once again, the Light Blues machine was misfiring. On a wet and windy afternoon, a goal in each half, from Keith Houchen and Mickey Weir, gave Hibs a 2-0 lead. Worse news was to follow when it was announced that Richard Gough had to go into hospital for a foot operation and could be out for a month.

The Skol Cup again provided some relief, though the 2-1 away win over Morton was hardly a convincing display. Rowan Alexander's opener for the Greenock side was balanced out by an opportunist Mark Walters goal just before the break, and Mark Pickering gifted 'Gers the winner with an own goal after 47 minutes.

The first Old Firm clash of the season came on 26 August at Parkhead. The weather was unseasonal, with a swirling wind and rain making life difficult for the players. In a hurly-burly match play swung from end to end. Terry Butcher's first goal of the season after just five minutes gave Rangers a lead they held only until the 20th minute, when Celtic's Polish striker Jacki Dziekanowski knocked in an equaliser.

There was no further scoring, and there were the Light Blues, right down at the foot of the Premier Division table, with Celtic and Aberdeen joint top on 5 points.

angers' 40th Championship Title

Brighter September

Skol Cup progress continued with a comfortable 3-0 victory at Hamilton over the Accies, the goals coming from Mark Walters (2) and Trevor Steven. Mo Johnston had now not scored in six competitive matches, but there was money talk again at Ibrox. Trevor Steven's fee was fixed by a tribunal at just over £1.5 million, and in a surprise move, striker Davie Dodds arrived from Aberdeen for £100,000.

There was no league action on the first Saturday of September due to World Cup matches the following week. Rangers players were involved and enjoyed mixed fortunes. Ally McCoist was in Yugoslavia with the Scotland team which went down 3-1 after taking a first-half lead through Gordon Durie — a setback to our hopes of qualifying for Italy. Terry Butcher was meanwhile doing his 'Captain Courageous' act for England, playing on despite a bad head cut as a 0-0 draw was fought out with Sweden.

Both were back in domestic action the next Saturday as Rangers took on Aberdeen at Ibrox, Butcher playing with a protective headband over his injury. And at last there was something for the fans to celebrate, the Light Blues winning 1-0 through a great header from Johnston in 54 minutes — his first Premier Division goal.

After this match the league table had a most unfamiliar look, with only two points separating all ten teams. Despite the win, Rangers were still bottom, on goal difference.

It was time for the European Cup to take over, with the home leg of the tie against Bayern Munich. With Chris Woods back in goal, Rangers had high hopes, and after Mark Walters had put the Light Blues ahead from the penalty spot in 25 minutes the stadium was buzzing.

Four minutes later things started to go wrong, Kogl hitting a swerving shot past Woods into the Rangers net. There was worse to follow as Thon, with a penalty, and Augenthaler, with a superb 30-yard drive, gave the German side an unassailable lead. It was Rangers' heaviest Euro-defeat at Ibrox for years, and Graeme Souness summed it up by saying: "It was a lesson for our players."

Football gives you little time to sit and mope — perhaps fortunately — and three days later the team were back on the park for a league match against Dundee. It turned out to be a thriller. McCoist gave Rangers the lead in 20 minutes with a tap-in goal, and that was it to half-time.

Dundee came out fighting, and in 62 minutes Albert Craig headed the equaliser. Ten minutes later Rangers were down to ten men as young defender Scott Nisbet was ordered off, but this merely spurred them on, and 'Super Ally' restored their lead with six minutes to go. Dundee refused to lie down, and Keith Wright snatched an equaliser in the last minute of the game.

Writing in *The Scotsman*, Denny McGee observed that "Rangers don't look like a team that cost £11 million", but at least the Light Blues were off the bottom of the table, a point ahead of Dunfermline.

There was no doubting the team's determination as they took the field for the Skol Cup semi-final against Dunfermline the following Wednesday. From the 11th minute, when Trevor Steven scored the opener, it was one-way traffic, and further goals from Johnston, McCoist (two) and Ian Ferguson took Rangers to their fourth Skol final in a row. Souness put things in perspective as usual, saying: "It's nice to be in another cup final, but my priority is always to win the Premier League."

League points were hard to come by, though, as the Light Blues found when they travelled to East End Park to face the 'Pars' for the second time in four days. It all started right, McCoist scoring a super goal in 12 minutes after a great through ball from Steven had put him clear.

But just three minutes later there was despair for Rangers as Ross Jack equalised — another controversial goal following a challenge on keeper Chris Woods, who was injured but able to carry on. All in all, a disappointing afternoon.

The last day of September saw Rangers improve their position with a 1-0 home league win over Hearts, Johnston's 35th minute strike proving enough to take the points. It was not a great match, and there was concern when Ian Ferguson had to go off injured, Davie Dodds coming on to make his debut for 'Gers. The team had moved up to 6th in the table, four points behind leaders Aberdeen.

Steady Progress

October 1989 saw steady progress on the league front, a cup disappointment, more international action for Ibrox stars, and a classic example of the 'Rangers Rumour' syndrome so prevalent in the press in recent years.

Mo's first league goal

The only Premier Division setback came in the month's first match, when a visit to Motherwell saw the Light Blues come away empty-handed, former Ibrox favourites doing most of the damage. With Mark Walters out through injury, Rangers never really sparked in attack and were always struggling after Bobby Russell latched on to a superb pass from Davie Cooper and rounded Bonny Ginzburg to place the ball into the net.

This win placed Motherwell — managed of course by ex-Ranger Tommy McLean — top of the Premier Division, at least for the next 24 hours. Graeme Souness was clearly disappointed, saying: "There was some bad finishing from Scotland's strike force (*McCoist and Johnston*). We made one mistake at the back and that cost us the game."

The following week, it was time for Scotland's strike force to do national duty again as, with Richard Gough, they flew out to Paris for a World Cup qualifier. Terry Butcher and Gary Stevens were meantime on the plane to Poland for England's equally important match in Katowice. Bonny Ginzburg was also called up for Israel's two-leg decider against Colombia.

The night before the big match, Scott Nisbet won another under-21 cap as the young Scots went down to their French counterparts 3-1. At least they scored a goal, which was more than the senior team could manage, a bad 3-0 defeat leaving Scotland needing a point from the last qualifying match against Norway at Hampden. It was nailbiting time again....

While all this was going on, Kevin Drinkell, a favourite with the fans during his spell at Ibrox, returned south to join Coventry City.

Premier Division action resumed with a home game against Dundee United. Mo Johnston opened the scoring, picking up the pieces in typical style in a goalmouth scramble after United keeper Billy Thomson had dropped a Walters header. Michael O'Neill equalised from the spot after Stuart Munro was adjudged to have handled, but Ally McCoist hit a brave winner with 15 minutes to go. He had insisted on playing on despite having five stitches put in a head cut. The match also saw Chris Woods return to first team action.

On 18 October, the papers were buzzing with the news that two Liverpool FC directors had been seen at Ibrox. There was an immediate jump to the conclusion that Graeme Souness was on his way and Kenny Dalglish would be taking over as manager. No truth in it — the men from Anfield were up in Glasgow to see the impressive facilities at Ibrox and talk over commercial activities with their Rangers counterparts.

Four days later, Rangers made the short journey to Hampden for the Skol Cup Final against the old rivals, Aberdeen. In a tense and exciting match the scores were tied at the end of 90 minutes. Paul Mason gave the Dons the lead in 22 minutes, the equaliser coming from a Mark Walters penalty 12 minutes later. Rangers exerted considerable pressure, and Johnston (twice) and Gary Stevens hit the woodwork, but Aberdeen held out.

Was it to be a penalty decider again, we wondered? It was not, but the cup went to the north-east, not back to Ibrox, Mason notching his second in the first period of extra time to the disappointment of the large Rangers contingent in the 61,000 crowd.

The Light Blues had two Premier Division matches scheduled for the following week, and came out of them with a 5-0 aggregate and fourth place in the table, just one point behind joint leaders Celtic and Aberdeen. Things were coming together at last.

The midweek 2-0 away victory over St Mirren, with goals from McCoist and Johnston, was notable for the impressive display of Ian McCall, who provided the pass for Mo's goal. Three days later the strike-force was at it again, two from Ally and one from Mo seeing Hibs off at Ibrox. All the goals came in the second half.

It was not all good news, however — Richard Gough fractured his cheekbone in the Hibs match and would be off for a month. Meanwhile Rangers were linked with yet another English player, the 19-year-old Exeter City fullback Chris Vinnicombe. The move went cool for a while when Exeter's estimate of the player's value turned out to be rather more than Rangers wanted to pay. He did join the club shortly afterwards.

Magic Strikes

November saw a trio of notable goals, and the departure of a player who has graced every team he played with, Rangers not excepted.

The first Saturday of the month saw the second Old Firm clash of the season, a match won by a Mo Johnston special — see our match report feature for all the details. The goal set Mo up for Scotland's vital World Cup tie with Norway at Hampden on 15 November, but it was his striking partner who was to steal the headlines, Ally's perfect lob over Thorstvedt into the net being enough, despite the scare of a late Norwegian equaliser, to ensure Scotland's place in the World Cup finals in Italy.

With World Cup euphoria still very much in the air, Rangers travelled to East End Park for a

15

Premier Division clash with Dunfermline. It was a tough encounter on a wet, slippery pitch. Dunfermline had three men booked and their midfielder Wes Saunders was sent off after 73 minutes for a bad foul on McCoist.

Mark Walters missed the resulting penalty, Tom Carson pulling off a fine save, but by then the Light Blues had the match well under control. After a goalless first half, Rangers went ahead with a Walters shot from a narrow angle in 51 minutes. McCoist hit a post two minutes later, and in 67 minutes Mo Johnston wrapped up the points with a low drive past Carson.

Rangers were now third in the table, equal on points with Aberdeen and Hearts, but there was a setback the following Wednesday when Aberdeen took the points 1-0 at Pittodrie with a superb goal from Dutch striker Hans Gillhaus — his third in two games since joining the Dons. It was a thrilling match, and manager Souness was clearly not too upset, saying: "If we play like that every week, we will win the Championship."

Sure enough, the following Saturday saw the Light Blues back on course with Johnston, Butcher and McCoist all finding the net against Dunfermline — and Mo missed a penalty too! McCoist's strike put 'Super Ally' level on 127 goals with Premier Division record-holder Frank McGarvey.

It was Ray Wilkins' last match for Rangers. The 34-year-old midfield ace, who had contributed so much in his time at Ibrox, was leaving for London to play for Queens Park Rangers. He made sure it was a memorable farewell, having a superb match in midfield and leaving the pitch to a great ovation from the Ibrox fans.

As 'Butch' went south, Nigel Spackman from QPR was on his way north, signing for Rangers in a half-million-pound deal. Looking forward to the new challenge, Nigel expressed his feelings by saying that "Rangers are one of biggest clubs in Europe."

Back To The Top

The dark days of December were lightened by an unbeaten spell in the league and Rangers' long-awaited return to the top of the Premier Division table — but there was a reverse at Ibrox as well.

The first Premier Division match of the month took the 'Gers travelling support to Tynecastle. They came away happy with the result, but a little less happy with the referee.

Eamonn Bannon's goal for Hearts was cancelled out by one of his colleagues, Dave McCreery

obligingly putting the ball in his own net. The winner was scored by Trevor Steven — one of a number of important goals he put his name to in the course of the season. The win put Rangers equal first in the table with Aberdeen after 16 games, but the celebrations were muted. Mark Walters was sent off in the match by referee Hugh Williamson and was suspended for three games.

The following week Rangers entertained Motherwell at Ibrox. An early goal from captain Butcher was all the 33,500 crowd had to cheer for most of the time — apart from a successful home debut by new boy Spackman. Most of the excitement was in the last ten minutes, as Rangers hit two superb goals. First Ally McCoist broke the Premier Division record with his 128th goal in the competition, and then John Brown stormed up from defence to put the third one away.

Before the next league game, Chris Woods appeared for England B against Yugoslavia — his first international for a year — and Terry Butcher was again in the senior squad. England won both these friendly matches 2-1.

Winter had set in for the trip to Tannadice. After overnight snow and frost the Saturday was a miserable day, windy and with cold rain. Mixu Paatalainen opened the scoring for United, the big Finn probably feeling quite at home in the conditions, and Rangers equalised through Mo Johnston after a Stuart Munro shot had rebounded from young keeper Alan Main — he was more than likely frozen at the time! With Aberdeen not playing, the point was enough to take the Light Blues clear at the top of the table.

There were unfamiliar visitors to Ibrox on 19 December. Arsenal, the English League champions, had arrived to play the Light Blues in the Zenith Challenge. On a very cold evening, the trophy went back to London, Mo Johnston's 50th minute effort being insufficient to match goals from Dixon and Quinn.

There were two more league fixtures before the end of the year. Davie Dodds, coming on as a sub, hit his first goal for Rangers to pip St Mirren at Ibrox, and over at Easter Road the teams fought out a goalless draw. Rangers' league record for the month was 8 points from 5 games, 7 goals against 2, and they could go into the New Year in good heart.

Starting the Nineties in Style

The new decade started in traditional style with the Old Firm match, this time at Parkhead. A tremendous crowd of over 54,000 enjoyed a tight tussle decided by a man playing in his first

Old Firm game. Nigel Spackman showed that he relished the occasion by striking a superb winner, finishing off a move that he started in midfield by continuing his run and sliding the ball past Pat Bonner in the Celtic goal.

This was the start of a magnificent Rangers run which can be seen in retrospect to have sewn up the Championship. Four days after the Celtic game, the first home game of the 90s, against Aberdeen in front of 41,000 people, was decisively settled by goals from Walters and McCoist to put the Light Blues convincingly clear at the top of the table.

There was no let-up the following week. Rangers were really on song now and bottom club Dundee were despatched 3-0. The McCoist/Johnston strike force bagged one each before Ally was replaced by Davie Dodds, rapidly becoming something of a Super Sub for the Light Blues. Davie picked up his second goal of the season to round things off. Rangers were now four points clear of Aberdeen and in 23 league matches had conceded a mere 12 goals.

Saturday 20 January brought a break from the league programme in the form of a 3rd Round Scottish Cup match against First Division pacemakers St Johnstone at Ibrox. There is always the memory of stumbles at this stage against the likes of Hamilton Accies and Berwick Rangers, but there was no faltering this time.

Mo Johnston made the break after just three minutes. Mo chested down a Stuart Munro cross and netted, keeper John Balavage seeming to pick the ball up late. John Brown and Mark Walters added second-half goals to take the Light Blues through, and there was great anticipation when the Fourth Round draw put the Old Firm together at Parkhead.

But that was a month ahead, and meantime there was an away match with Dunfermline to concentrate on. The usual great travelling support boosted the East End Park crowd to 17,350 and Gary Stevens, an ever-present in the team, rewarded them with his first goal of the season. In their past seven matches, Rangers had won six and drawn one, scoring eleven goals and conceding not one — a great tribute to the defence and to Chris Woods in particular.

Fine Times in February

February's first action came in a league match at Ibrox, Dundee United being the visitors. Rangers came out raring to go, with Chris Vinnicombe included in the starting line-up for the first time.

Ally McCoist came close with two early chances

before Rangers struck gold three times in 20 minutes. First it was Mark Walters receiving an inch-perfect pass from McCoist and smacking the ball left-footed into the net well out of Andy Main's reach. Then Mo Johnston reacted quickly to return a poor clearance to McCoist, who netted without hesitation. And just two minutes later Johnston himself finished off a four-man move to give Rangers a healthy three-goal lead with only 39 minutes played.

There was another goal to come before half-time — and it was the first Chris Woods had conceded in 602 minutes of football. The scorer was John Clark with a header.

That was the end of the scoring but the Light Blues stayed on top and could easily have added a couple more. Walters went off with 20 minutes to go, Sandy Robertson taking his place for his first taste of senior action for nearly a year.

McCoist's goal put him on 131 in league matches, equalling Rangers' postwar record. It was some time before he made that mark his own. Rangers were now seven points clear and Graeme Souness was delighted. "Our finishing was absolutely brilliant," he said.

The following Saturday was a good one for two Rangers players. Mo Johnston scored the goal which levelled the scores at Motherwell and kept the long unbeaten run going, and Ian Durrant made his comeback for Rangers Reserves in a League Cup tie against Hearts at Ibrox.

Durrant's standing with the fans is shown by the size of the crowd — 6000 turned out to welcome him back to competitive action after 16 long months out through injury. Ian, made captain for the day, had a goal disallowed and then scored from the spot as the match went into a penalty shoot-out. Unfortunately there was no happy ending, Hearts winning on penalties 7-6, but Ian clearly felt great to be back.

There were contrasting honours for two Rangers men, both equally welcome. Graeme Souness took the Tennents Manager of the Month Award and Mo Johnston was voted Newcomer of the Year by Stenhouse Rangers Supporters Club — an award he accepted graciously. The following week, consistent Stuart Munro had his turn, being voted B&Q Player of the Month for his fine displays at full-back. Meanwhile, Derek Ferguson travelled east to join Dundee on an extended loan.

Back on the park, a scrappy game played in very wet conditions ended in a 0-0 draw with Hearts at Ibrox; but minds were concentrating on the clash with Celtic. It was, sadly, to provide

another Cup disappointment for the Light Blues.

Tommy Coyne's first competitive goal for four months, knocked in after Chris Woods had parried a shot from Joe Miller, was enough to put Rangers out of the Cup for another year. The match was played in very muddy conditions, and Graeme Souness said afterwards: "It wasn't a game for footballers." It was Rangers' first defeat since 22 November.

Springing on to Glory

March was an undistinguished month. The weather didn't improve much, and on the pitch things were never quite right. A visit to Dens Park produced a 2-2 draw against a Dundee side fighting desperately against relegation, the goals coming from Dodds and Johnston. Saturday 10 March was blank, then the short trip to Paisley produced a point but no goals against a determined St Mirren defence, Scott Nisbet making a rare first-team appearance in the no 9 shirt.

Hibernian came to Ibrox next, and went back to Edinburgh having stolen a 1-0 victory in front of 36,500 people. Rangers were still six points clear, but Graeme Souness refused to accept that the Championship was safe. There were six matches to go, the first of them being the final Old Firm clash of the season, at Ibrox on Saturday 1 April. Our match report feature tells the story of a decisive 3-0 victory.

Every match mattered now, and the following Saturday the Light Blues took the road to Pittodrie to face Aberdeen, who were six points behind them and still held on to a flickering hope that Rangers could be caught. It was vital to come away from what is always a tough match with at least a point, and that was achieved. A goalless draw at Pittodrie at that stage of the season can definitely be seen as a point gained and not a point dropped.

It was not an easy match for Rangers. Within 20 minutes they had lost both Gary Stevens and Ian Ferguson through injury, John Brown and Davie Dodds coming on as substitutes, but the Light Blues still created more chances than the Dons, though Dutch dangerman Hans Gillhaus had to be watched carefully — Rangers remembered only too well his spectacular goal on their last visit to Pittodrie. But the Ibrox team held out, and edged a little closer to the title. Four games left...

The next game was at home to Motherwell, a team who had caused 'Gers trouble earlier in the season. After an edgy first half in which several good chances were spurned, things really livened up in a frenetic spell from the 57th to the 65th minutes of the match.

First, Dodds was substituted by Derek Ferguson, back from his loan period with Dundee and making his first appearance since September. He got a great reception from the 39,300 crowd. Derek must have wondered what sort of match he had come into: a minute after he came on, Terry Butcher conceded a free-kick and had his name taken.

There was a familiar man behind the ball: Davie Cooper, a free-kick specialist. Davie has lost none of his skill, and he curled in a beauty for Neil Cusack to head home the opener. From the restart Rangers went straight for goal. Walters crossed and McCoist found himself competing with Trevor Steven for the ball. The midfielder won, volleying in a spectacular goal.

Five minutes later, John Brown went off, to be replaced by Scott Nisbet, who immediately got in a cross which fell to Mo Johnston. The striker reacted superbly, slipping the ball past the advancing Maxwell for the winner. With three matches left, Rangers were six points ahead of the pack, needing just one more point to be certain of lifting the trophy.

The great moment came in the 58th minute of the game at Tannadice on 21 April. A header from Trevor Steven did the job, and Rangers were the Champions of Scotland for the 40th time. The tremendous spirit in the club is shown by the fact that Woods, Gough and Brown all played when less than 100%, and Gary Stevens made an extra effort to return after a nasty injury to take his place at right-back.

Saturday 28 April 1990 was both a great day and a sad one. For the last home game of the season, Dunfermline provided the opposition. They were celebrating too — Jim Leishman's side had succeeded in staying in the Premier Division, at the expense of Dundee. But it was always going to be Rangers' party.

The Light Blues were in command from the start, and after Ally McCoist had scored a typical goal, it was a fiesta in the sunshine with a very special moment after 70 minutes when Graeme Souness came off the bench for not just his sole appearance of the season, but his very last run out as a player.

The crowd of over 40,000 gave 'the Gaffer' a fantastic reception, and the team responded by playing some delightful football, the reward being a Davie Dodds goal in the final minute of the match. Graeme was presented with the Championship trophy, there was the traditional lap of honour, and then he was gone. Afterwards he said: "I wish I was just beginning again, but when I think of players like Ian

Durrant, who is still out of the game through injury, I realise how lucky I've been."

The final seal of approval came from McEwans Lager, who announced an ongoing sponsorship deal with Rangers worth some £6m over the next six years. The celebrations were well and truly under way, but there was still one game to be played, and it too provided a very special moment.

The last match of the 1989-90 season was away to Hearts. The home side took the lead after 13 minutes when Chris Woods was adjudged to have fouled John Colquhoun, and John Robertson scored from the penalty spot. Four minutes later Rangers left-back Stuart Munro dispossessed Craig Levein and charged off upfield.

Normally in this situation Stuart would look for someone to pass to, or perhaps carry on to try to get in a telling cross. Not this time: he went

straight for goal and rammed a firm shot past Hearts keeper Henry Smith. Stuart played in every one of 'Gers 45 games last season and this was his only goal — what a time to get it!

There was no further scoring and the season ended, perhaps appropriately, with the ball in the hands of Chris Woods, the Premier Division's top goalkeeper and one of the inspirations behind Rangers' title success. Consistency was the key: as well as Stuart Munro, Mo Johnston also played in every match, Gary Stevens missed only one, Trevor Steven and Terry Butcher just two.

A settled team is more likely to be a successful one, and that's how it worked out. Now we wait to see what season 1990-91 produces. Rangers will be going for a third Championship in a row, but Cup success either at home or in Europe would be particularly sweet. We shall know all the answers next May!

Trevor Steven's championship-winning goal at Tannadice

Champions Again!

RANGERS
v Moscow Dynamo, Nov. 1945

Russian cameramen outside Ibrox

The Russians Are Coming!

As life slowly returned to normal after the end of World War Two in May 1945, there was naturally great eagerness among supporters to see big matches again. It was not possible to get the League programme going in time for a 1945-46 season, but every effort was made to provide entertainment for the fans, and there was tremendous anticipation when it was learned that the crack Russian side, Moscow Dynamo, would visit Glasgow for a match against Rangers at the end of their tour of Britain.

The match was scheduled for Wednesday 28 November 1945, with a kick-off time of 2.15, and with a capacity all-ticket crowd of 90,000 packed into the ground, there must have been many a business facing a temporary labour shortage that day! The *Glasgow Herald* reported with disapproval that 3/6d enclosure tickets (17.5p equivalent) were being sold outside the ground for £1.

The Russians had proved they could play. They had drawn with Chelsea in a dramatic match played in a thick London fog, travelled to Wales and thrashed Cardiff City 10-1, and then beaten a fancied Arsenal side which included the two great Blackpool players, Stanley Matthews and Stan Mortensen, as guests. So they arrived at Ibrox with an unbeaten record to defend.

The Rangers side included several players nearing the end of distinguished playing careers at Ibrox, including goalkeeper Jerry Dawson, full-back David Gray, and left-half Scot Symon, who was later to manage the club. New faces from the pre-war years included the great centre-half George Young, signed from Kirkintilloch Rob Roy in 1942, and the highly talented Torry Gillick at inside-forward. Torry played for Rangers from 1933 to 1935 and then went to Everton, returning to Ibrox in 1945. Dynamo were into the action early, warming up

on the pitch for 15 minutes before the kick-off. It looked to be the right tactic as they dominated the first quarter's play, showing outstanding control and speed both on and off the ball.

Within two minutes, the Moscow side were ahead. They were awarded a free-kick 20 yards from goal and their no 8, Kartsev, crashed the ball past Dawson into the net.

It seemed that Rangers must equalise five minutes later when Billy Williamson was fouled in the box — penalty! Up stepped Rangers right-winger Willie Waddell, but the Russian goalkeeper, 'Tiger' Khomich, who had an outstanding match, tipped the ball onto the bar and it was cleared to safety.

Dynamo continued to press forward at every opportunity, their wing-halves Blinkov and Oreshkin supporting the attack superbly well, and it was no real surprise when Kartsev finished off a wonderful passing move by scoring his second after 24 minutes.

Rangers showed great fighting spirit, however, and their reply was immediate. In a goalmouth scramble resulting from a long clearance by Jock Shaw, centre-forward Jimmy Smith got the vital touch past Khomich to reduce the arrears. Smith was injured in scoring the goal and was later replaced by Jimmy Duncanson.

There was no further scoring before half-time, but Rangers were beginning to hold the Russian side. Could they turn the match in the second half?

At one point Rangers found themselves a man down as well as a goal down. Dementiev was sent on as a sub for Bobrov without the Russian no 10 realising he had to go off, and for a few minutes Dynamo played with 12 men on the park!

Rangers came into the game more and more as the second half went on, with wingers Waddell and Johnstone tormenting the Russian defence.

The pressure told when Johnstone was brought down in the box. After consulting a linesman, the English referee, Mr Thompson from Leamington, awarded Rangers penalty no 2.

This time big George Young came forward to take the kick and made no mistake, thumping the ball into the net past Khomich to give Rangers a draw they fully deserved.

It had been a great day for football in Glasgow and at Ibrox, and it heralded the start of a wonderful period for the Light Blues. In the following seven years they won the Championship four times, finishing second on the other three occasions, did the hat-trick of three Scottish Cup wins in a row, and took the League Cup twice as well.

But no-one who was there will ever forget the match against Moscow Dynamo on a November day in 1945. The *Glasgow Herald* match report described it as "football at its best" and concluded: "Had the home side had five scoring forwards they would have won; but it must be admitted that from the spectators' point of view the Russian play was the more attractive" — a curious presentiment of a match that was to take place 27 years later.

Teams: *Rangers*: Jerry Dawson; David Gray, Jock Shaw (capt); Charlie Watkins, George Young, Scot Symon; Willie Waddell, Torry Gillick, Jimmy Smith (sub: Jimmy Duncanson), Billy Williamson, Charlie Johnstone.
Moscow Dynamo: Khomich; Radikorsky, Stankevich; Blinkov, Semichastny (capt), Oreshkin; Archangelski, Kartsev, Beskov, Bobrov (sub: Dementiev), Soloviev.

Pick of the Season
RANGERS *v Celtic*

HISTORY was in the making that cold November day. The Rangers supporters knew that sooner or later Mo Johnston would score against Celtic. Mo knew it too. It was inevitable. But nobody could have envisaged that it would happen in such dramatic and stunning fashion.

Rangers had completely dominated the first half of a match from which, it seemed, Celtic would be happy to take a point. The second period was drawing to a close with the stalemate still unbroken, although Coyne had hit the post during a rare Celtic attack when it seemed easier to score.

Rangers 1 — Celtic 0, November 1989

But with only two minutes to play, the drama unfolded:

Mark Walters, positioned centrally inside Celtic's half, picked up a Stuart Munro pass and pushed the ball out onto the wing to Mo Johnston, who slipped a pass to Ray Wilkins. The midfield general immediately involved Gary Stevens, who had taken up overlap position on the right flank.

The defender's subsequent cross into the Celtic box was only partially cleared by Chris Morris. Mo Johnston, hovering just outside the area, controlled the loose ball and struck a sweet low right foot shot that nestled in the Celtic net at Pat Bonner's right hand side, despite a despairing dive by the Irish keeper.

It is said that a picture paints a thousand words. The look of total joy on Mo's face said it all as he ran to the Rangers faithful to acknowledge their acclaim. Moments later he was engulfed by his jubilant team mates before continuing behind Bonner's goal to extend the celebration of his own personal triumph.

This earned Mo his first caution of the season but it didn't seem to matter as the striker's goal had taken Rangers to the top of the Premier Division (with 12 points) for the first, but not last, time that season. The victory and the day was his.

Many would say that the 1989-90 season was his as well.

WILLIE WADDELL

Willie Waddell was born in 1921 in the Lanarkshire village of Forth. Rangers signed him as a schoolboy and he made his first-team debut at the age of 17 in a 1938 pre-season friendly against Arsenal. It was a sensational start to what was to be a sensational career, Waddell scoring the only goal of the game and giving the current England left-back, Ernie Hapgood, a most uncomfortable afternoon.

In the 1938-39 season, Rangers dominated the League, losing only four out of 38 games and scoring 112 times as they swept to the title. It should have been the start of great things for Waddell, but like so much else in life, it was interrupted by the War.

Waddell stayed in Scotland and helped Rangers to win the Southern League Championship, as it was called, six seasons running. He also collected ten wartime caps for Scotland. By 1945, Waddell was an established member of the Rangers side, and would remain so until his playing days ended in 1956.

During his career Willie Waddell played 558 first-team games for Rangers. He scored 143 goals from the right wing but supplied many more, particularly for Willie Thornton, the two proving a deadly combination. There were five more Championship medals, in 1947, 1949, 1950, 1953 and his final year, 1956; a hat-trick of Cup wins in 1948-49-50 and another in 1953; and two successes in the League Cup.

Willie Waddell delighted the fans at Ibrox with his skilful play. With him in the no 7 jersey, Rangers knew that they could rely on a good number of chances being created — there were few fullbacks who could hold him. He took his total of Scottish caps to 27.

Waddell retired the year before Rangers played in Europe for the first time, but he was to get to know the European scene before too many years had passed. After leaving Rangers, he went on to manage Kilmarnock, taking them to the League championship and a Scottish Cup final against Rangers in 1961, when the Light Blues won 2-0. There was also a memorable Cup semi-final in 1966 in which Rangers defeated Kilmarnock 6-4.

In November 1969, Rangers went out of the European Cup 6-2 on aggregate to Gornik of Poland. It was the end for Davie White, the

manager. He was dismissed and after a short period with Willie Thornton in temporary charge, Willie Waddell was back at Ibrox, in charge of the club he had served so well as a player.

He was manager for just two and a half years, at a time when Celtic were dominating the scene in Scotland. Ironically, that domination led to Rangers' greatest success. The 1971 Scottish Cup Final was an Old Firm clash. The first match ended in a draw, Derek Johnstone scoring with three minutes to go after coming on as a substitute.

For the replay, Rangers lost Alex Miller through injury and drafted in Jim Denny for his senior debut. There was to be no fairytale, however, Celtic winning 2-1. But as the Parkhead club were already in the European Cup as League champions, Rangers took their place in the Cup-Winners Cup, and went on to win it, as is told elsewhere in this annual.

It was the highlight of Willie Waddell's period in charge of the team. Shortly after that famous victory he moved 'upstairs' as general manager of the club, Jock Wallace taking over the reins from him.

Mo scoring his first Premier League goal

ALLY McCOIST

'Super Ally', a Bellshill lad, is in his 8th season with the Light Blues — and he's still only 27. Ally's professional career started with St Johnstone and he very quickly made his mark. John Greig tried to sign him for Rangers in summer 1981, but Sunderland offered a higher fee to the Perth club, and Ally headed south.

Two years later he was back, one of Greig's last signings as manager, and surely one of his best. He was into the goals before long and finished as the club's top scorer with 22 in that first season, including a dramatic hat-trick in the League Cup triumph over Celtic, Rangers taking the match 3-2 after extra time.

Ally McCoist has continued to put the ball where he most likes to see it — in the back of the opposition net

— with consistency ever since. In Graeme Souness's first full season, 1986-87, Ally and his striking partner Robert Fleck put 64 goals away between them.

Ally has played up front with a variety of fellow-strikers, including Fleck (they were known as Butch Cassidy and the Sundance Kid), Mark Falco and Kevin Drinkell, but has surely found the perfect foil in Mo Johnston. The two are not only Rangers' first-choice front line but also a regular pairing for Scotland. Johnston's goals in the World Cup campaign were vital, and it was of course 'Super Ally' who scored the goal against Norway at Hampden which finally took Scotland to Italy.

On 9th December 1989, Ally's goal against Motherwell took his Premier Division total to 128, surpassing the record previously held by Celtic's Frank McGarvey. Always able to take a joke against himself, Ally said: "If I could head the ball I would have taken the record much earlier!"

He is a deadly finisher with either foot and has the natural striker's ability to appear in the danger area at just the right time, but it has to be admitted that he is not the world's greatest header of a ball. With his other talents, that hardly seems to matter.

Apart from a bad hamstring injury that kept him out for three months in the 1988-89 season, Ally has kept fairly well clear of serious injury problems. Last season he appeared in 37 of the Light Blues' 45 matches, hitting the net 19 times to again end up as top scorer.

A great favourite with the fans on and off the field, Ally McCoist has a lively personality and is a renowned practical joker. The stories about him are legion. Derek Johnstone, another great Rangers striker, is said to have called McCoist 'Ally Two-Caps' after he made his Scotland debut against Holland, remarking: "That's you got two caps, Ally — your first and your last!" The joke's on Big Derek now as Ally adds steadily to his appearances in the dark blue jersey.

But there's no joking in front of goal, particularly among opposing defenders when 'Super Ally' is around. He's set to put away a lot more goals for Rangers yet.

THE SOUNESS YEARS

A Lot Has Happened Since April '86 ...

Tuesday 8 April 1986 was a significant day — not just for Rangers but for the whole footballing world. On that day it was announced at a press conference at Ibrox that Graeme Souness, the current Scottish team captain, would be leaving the Italian club Sampdoria to join Rangers as player/manager.

Souness was a month away from his 33rd birthday. After a highly successful career at Liverpool, where he was club captain and with the club won five league championship medals and three European Cups, he had moved to Sampdoria two years previously, taking his new club to an Italian Cup triumph and becoming a great favourite with the Italian fans.

Despite being born in Edinburgh, Graeme Souness had never played for a Scottish club: before Liverpool he was with Spurs and Middlesbrough. Now, at a time when most of his thoughts must have been directed towards Scotland's summer World Cup campaign in Mexico, he had landed probably the top job in Scottish football.

He arrived at a time when Rangers were desperate for success. The last Championship win was back in 1978, and in the four seasons before Souness took over, Rangers' highest league position was fourth. The Scottish Cup had not been won since 1981.

This was not the kind of record that Rangers were used to and David Holmes, the man brought in by chairman Lawrence Marlborough as chief executive, was given the task of finding a replacement for Jock Wallace as manager. He said later: "I sat down to make a list and Graeme Souness was the first name I put on it. I didn't go any further."

The immediate priority was to qualify for the UEFA Cup the following season. Rangers scraped in by beating Motherwell 2-0 in the last league match of the 1985-86 campaign. By then Souness had a top-class man by his side. Walter Smith arrived from Dundee United to be assistant manager: he had the vital experience of Premier Division football which Souness lacked.

Summer In Mexico

With the domestic season over, Souness had two aims: to lead Scotland to success in Mexico and to start rebuilding the Rangers team for the following season. Light Blues fans soon realised that this meant buying the best players available — regardless of where they came from.

The first public signing was striker Colin West, lifted from Watford for £200,000. But in fact Souness had already secured a signature he very much wanted. It was a four-year contract and the name on the dotted line was Ally McCoist, Rangers' top young striker. The contract included a signing-on fee, something new for the Ibrox club but which Souness knew was essential if he was to get key players to join him.

Among the sports writers in Mexico with the Scottish team, there was almost more interest in who Rangers were going to sign next than in the team's performances. Rumours flew around — a trend that has continued to this day as far as Graeme Souness and Rangers are concerned! One day it might be England goalkeeper Peter Shilton joining the club, the next the star Brazilian Falcao. Souness played along with the game, telling journalists: "I have had satisfying talks with a big-name player. He is involved in the World Cup but I can't name him at the moment."

The mystery man turned out to be Chris Woods, then of Norwich City and England's no 2 goalkeeper. The fee was £600,000 — a record for a goalkeeper at the time — and Chris has turned out to be one of Souness's best signings. He may not have realised it, but he was far from the first top English goalkeeper to come to Rangers — the club signed Herbert Lock from Southampton in 1908!

If Woods was a great catch, the next Ibrox new boy was even greater. Graeme Souness knew that he needed a new captain and he also knew the man he wanted. He followed the East Anglia trail again and returned with his prize — Terry Butcher of Ipswich and England, signed for £725,000.

It was a signing described by David Holmes as "a stroke of genius" and no Light Blues fan would disagree. Big Terry — an unmistakeable figure at 6'4" — settled in straight away and has been an inspiring leader on the field and an immensely popular figure off it ever since.

The First Title

Graeme Souness must surely still wake up sometimes in a cold sweat thinking about his first taste of Premier Division action. Saturday 9 August 1986 could hardly have been a less auspicious opener, for the player/manager or for the club.

The game was against Hibs at Easter Road. For Souness it lasted 36 minutes. He was ordered off

with his son, Jordan

by referee Mike Delaney for a bad foul on George McCluskey. Worse was to follow when mayhem broke out on the pitch involving every player on both sides except Hibs keeper Alan Rough. And when football did resume, Rangers lost the match 1-2.

Souness had realised he would be a marked man, but he was determined there would be no intimidation. After the match he said: "I was out of order at Easter Road, but other teams are going to be aggressive because we are the side everyone wants to beat...we have to match other teams physically and I will not change that attitude."

There was a return to something like normality in the next match, a 1-0 home win over Falkirk which brought another new face to the Ibrox line-up. Actually it was a well-kent face — the Northern Ireland international full-back Jimmy Nicholl, who had rejoined the club in a swap deal which took striker Bobby Williamson to West Bromwich Albion.

Before long there were more changes, Iain Ferguson and John MacDonald leaving. On the field, the League Cup (now renamed the Skol Cup) provided some relief, as it so often has. Wins over Stenhousemuir, East Fife (after a penalty shoot-out at Methil), and both Dundee teams brought Rangers to a final against Celtic.

Souness was absent injured but the team rose to the occasion and gave him his first trophy, beating their oldest rivals 2-1 with goals from Ian Durrant and Davie Cooper. By then Rangers were into the third round of the UEFA Cup with wins over Ilves Tampere of Finland and the Portuguese side Boavista Porto. But there was to be no European glory this time around, an away goal taking Borussia Moenchengladbach through after a tough second game in Germany in which Cooper and Stuart Munro were sent off.

Souness could now concentrate on the league campaign. He has always said that the Premier Division championship means more to him than any other title; he also said that he did not expect to win it in his first season with the club.

There was steady improvement in the months that followed. In the week before Christmas Souness made another important signing, bringing the powerful defender Graham Roberts from Spurs for £450,000. The traditional Ne'er Day Old Firm match was vital if Rangers were to catch Celtic, who were leading the title chase. Souness had a superb match in midfield, Roberts fitted in well beside Terry Butcher, and the striking partnership of Fleck and McCoist provided the goals to give the Light Blues a 2-0 victory.

This was Chris Woods' eighth game in a row

without a goal conceded. He was to go on to break the British record of 1,196 minutes, but the goal that finally ended the long run brought one of the most surprising results of the season.

Graeme Souness's first Scottish Cup tie was almost as much of a nightmare as his first league match. The opponents were Hamilton, bottom of the Premier Division and already beaten by Rangers three times that season. It was fourth time lucky for the Accies as a 70th minute Adrian Sprott goal dumped the Light Blues out of the cup.

The team reacted with determination and style, scoring eight goals in their next two league matches to put things firmly back on course. March brought five wins in five games, and despite losing the last Old Firm game 3-1, by the end of April Rangers were within touching distance of the title. A Terry Butcher goal at Pittodrie gave it to them, and they could turn the last home game of the season, against St Mirren, into a gala day. Robert Fleck provided the goal to round it all off, and the celebrations started in earnest.

Rangers Revolution

The season had been significant in many ways. As well as bringing Rangers their first title since 1978, there had been a revolution off the field. Graeme Souness is a winner and a man with style, and he wanted Rangers Football Club to have style from top to bottom.

The players were given new guidelines on dress and behaviour, and the stadium — already vastly improved in the previous decade — saw further refinements, including executive suites for corporate entertainment, a top-class restaurant, and conference facilities including rental of the club's legendary Blue Room.

The fans realised that something special was starting to happen, and attendances soared. The game against Hearts on 25 April 1987 saw the millionth paying customer of the season pass through the Ibrox turnstiles — nearly 100,000 more than Manchester United registered and ensuring that there would be more money available for forays into the transfer market.

Reflecting on his first year, the player/manager said: "On about five occasions this season, Rangers have played — for ten minutes — football somewhere near a good Liverpool team. The difference is that Liverpool do it for 75 minutes a match, 42 games a season." There was clearly some way to go before the revolution was completed.

Winning the title meant two things. It meant entry to the European Cup, and it meant that the fans would expect this level of success to

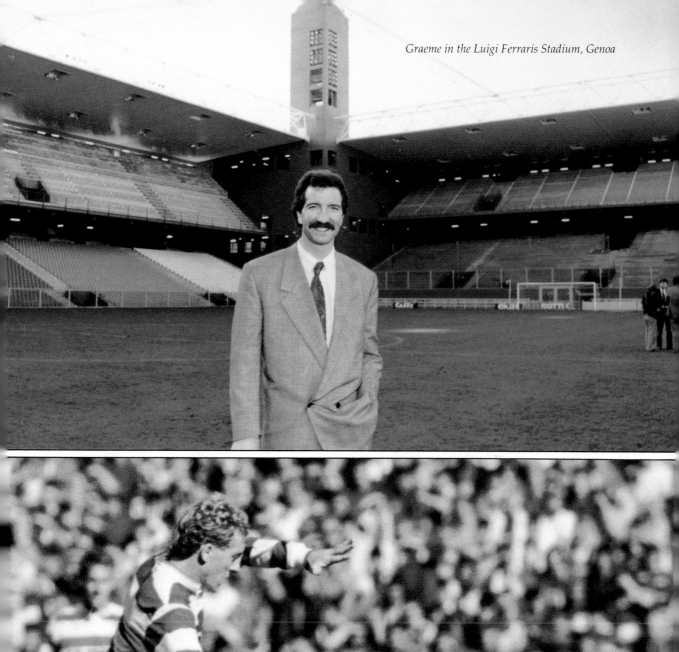

Graeme in the Luigi Ferraris Stadium, Genoa

continue. With this in mind, there was further transfer activity in the summer of 1987. In came Avi Cohen, John MacGregor and Mark Falco, and out went Bobby Russell, Neil Woods — a signing during the previous season who never settled at Ibrox — and Ally Dawson.

Down To Earth

You no sooner go up in football than you come down again, and season 1987-88 was to prove that fortune is a fickle thing indeed. With Butcher, Roberts and Souness himself unable to play in the first two games of the season through suspension, the team struggled, and league progress was hard to come by.

Once again there was better luck in the Skol Cup, with a particularly impressive 4-1 win over Hearts producing just the kind of flowing football Graeme Souness was seeking. Semi-final success against Motherwell brought Rangers to their second final in a row, against Aberdeen this time.

By now Colin West, Graeme Souness's first big-money capture, had departed for Sheffield Wednesday and there were two more arrivals — Ian McCall from Dunfermline and the vastly experienced Trevor Francis, a close friend of the player/manager's, from Atalanta.

The European experience which both Souness and Francis had accumulated over many years was put to the test on 30 September as Rangers lined up for the second leg of the European Cup tie with Dynamo Kiev. They had held the Russian club to 1-0 in the away leg: could they turn the tie around at Ibrox?

The stadium was packed and the atmosphere was electric. Rangers were inspired and before half-time Mark Falco had levelled the scores. The moment all of Ibrox was waiting for came early in the second half. A Francis cross, a Falco header and Ally McCoist applied the finishing touch. Rangers were through to the second round.

October was a month of mixed fortunes. Woods and Butcher were sent off, with Celtic's Frank McAvennie, in a drawn Old Firm match, and there was the most expensive dip so far into the transfer market when Souness bought Richard Gough, whose play he had long admired, from Spurs for £1.1 million.

Gough repaid some of the fee almost straight away, in a superb Skol Cup final shown live on television. It was 1-0 to Aberdeen then 2-1 to Rangers, Cooper and Durrant scoring, then 3-2 to Aberdeen before Robert Fleck scored a dramatic late equaliser to take the match into extra time. No more goals meant a penalty

shoot-out and Aberdeen's Peter Nicholas was the unfortunate man to miss. Rangers had taken the trophy again.

That was to be the high spot of the season on the pitch. After beating Gornik of Poland, Rangers were eliminated from the European Cup by the Romanian champions Steaua Bucharest. By then they were playing without Terry Butcher, who broke his leg in November and was out for the rest of the season — a serious setback for the club. Graham Roberts took over as captain. And there was yet another aberration in the Scottish Cup, the Light Blues losing to Dunfermline in the fourth round.

While all this was going on, players were arriving or leaving at such a rate that it was sometimes hard to keep up. Mark Falco and Robert Fleck were both transferred to English clubs; in their place came two more exciting acquisitions, the vastly experienced Ray Wilkins and Mark Walters from Aston Villa, the first black player to appear in the Premier Division and a firm favourite with the Ibrox crowd. John Brown came from Dundee and defender Jan Bartram from Denmark. His was to be a brief stay only.

With all this restructuring going on — and it can all be seen as part of Graeme Souness's long-term plans for the club — it was perhaps hardly surprising that league form was inconsistent. Rangers' success the previous season had served to spur on their great rivals from across the city, and Celtic were determined to prove a point.

They did so in emphatic style, landing the league and cup double. Souness would be under even greater pressure in season 1988-89 to restore Rangers to winning ways, especially in the Premier Division.

Back To The Top

To no-one's real surprise, there were further changes before the start of the new season. Jan Bartram returned to Denmark and Graham Roberts went back to London to play for Chelsea — a move made inevitable after a disagreement between the player and his manager became public at the end of the previous season. Roberts had been popular with the fans and many were sorry to see him go.

In came striker Kevin Drinkell, another East Anglian capture, signed from Norwich for £500,000. Few had heard of Drinkell before Souness signed him, but it proved to be a shrewd investment. And there was yet another England international in the team for the start of the Premier Division campaign.

Instead of a tour, Rangers went to Italy for pre-

season training, a trip aimed both at providing the players with an enjoyable environment in which to work and an encouragement to get down to business. Tough training sessions in the sun were the order of the day, and none trained harder than Terry Butcher, working his way back to fitness after his long lay-off.

Souness's 'Italian job' was to sign defender Gary Stevens from Everton for £1 million. He joined the squad in the sunshine and was to play a decisive role in the season ahead as Rangers strove to regain the league title.

This time there were no nightmare openings. The first game was won 2-0, Stevens and Ally McCoist providing the goals to defeat Hamilton Accies, and in eight league matches Rangers dropped only one point. The run included the famous 5-1 victory over Celtic which we feature in a special match report. Wilkins, Drinkell and Walters all scored in that match and it seemed that the team was settling into real consistency, playing the kind of football that Souness wanted to see.

The Skol Cup followed a familiar pattern, enjoyable midweek matches with plenty of goals taking the Light Blues to their third final in a row. Before the final, again with Aberdeen as the opponents, veteran striker Andy Gray, a self-confessed lifelong Rangers fan, joined the

club, to his own huge delight, as cover for Drinkell and McCoist, but there was a bitter blow for Ian Durrant, when he suffered a very serious knee injury which was to put him out of football for over a year.

The Skol Cup Final was another classic watched by a large TV audience as well as a crowd of 72,000 at Hampden Park. Rangers took the title 3-2 thanks to a late McCoist goal and again hopes of the treble of Skol Cup, league and Scottish Cup were raised.
The only blemish on the season was an early exit from the European Cup at the hands of Cologne. Success in that arena was proving the most difficult of all to achieve.

Two further injuries showed the wisdom of providing quality cover for every position on the field. Ally McCoist was sidelined for two months with a hamstring injury and Chris Woods went down with labyrinthitis, a rare infection which affects the balance. He was to be out until February, giving Nicky Walker the chance of an extended run in the first team. He proved a very capable deputy for the England keeper.

Before Christmas there was further sensation off the field when chairman Lawrence Marlborough sold his controlling interest in the club to David Murray, head of Murray International and a close friend of Graeme Souness. The two men are only a year apart in age and similar in their outlook on life: both have a burning desire for success and drive themselves 100% to achieve it.

Not only did David Murray take over as chairman, Graeme Souness became a director of Rangers with a 10% stake in the club. Two young men still in their mid-thirties were to take the great old club forward into the 1990s, giving it total commitment and demanding the same from everybody else.

On the field, the Premier Division campaign was proceeding well. Defeat by Motherwell in early January served merely as a spur and Rangers were unbeaten in 12 games after that, including their first Old Firm league win at Parkhead for nine years. Woods and McCoist were back in the side, and in form, and the Scottish Cup campaign was for once going well, despite another near-disaster in the third round when Raith Rovers held the Light Blues to a draw at Starks Park.

The replay was won 3-0 and Stranraer were summarily despatched 8-0 in the fourth round. Replay victories over Dundee United and a very gallant St Johnstone side took Rangers to a final clash with Celtic.

Before then, a home match against Hearts on 29 April brought the title — the prize Graeme Souness still rates highest — back to Ibrox. The team for that 4-0 victory included two more new signings, Mel Sterland from Sheffield Wednesday, who scored two of the goals, the other two going to Kevin Drinkell, and teenager Tom Cowan, bought from Clyde for £100,000.

Evidence of how far the Rangers Revolution had progressed is shown by the starting lineup that day. It read: **Woods**, **Stevens**, Munro, Gough, **Wilkins**, **Butcher**, **Drinkell**, **Sterland**, McCoist, **Walters**, Derek Ferguson. The names in bold type — 7 out of 11 — are all English players brought to Ibrox by Graeme Souness. Cowan and Davie Cooper were the substitutes.

The end-of-season party was spoiled twice. In the last league match at Ibrox, Aberdeen were mean enough to try to the extent that they won 3-0; Rangers could be excused for having their minds on the Cup Final the following week. Two incidents from the game serve to show Graeme Souness's attention to detail.

First he got hold of the match ball and presented it to the youngest fan he could find — a very special present! — and then he led Ian Durrant, still on crutches, onto the pitch to join the rest of the players in the celebrations as League President Jack Steedman presented the trophy to Terry Butcher.

There were, unfortunately, to be no celebrations the following week. The day was superb, the setting perfect, and the 72,000 Hampden crowd looked forward to a great match. Rangers were without Ray Wilkins, who had been such an inspiration, but Souness named himself as a substitute.

The match was a disappointment, and the single goal somehow summed it all up. Near the end of the first half, Gary Stevens, one of Rangers' most consistent performers throughout the whole season, mistimed a pass-back. Joe Miller pounced and his shot flew past Woods into the net.

Souness put himself and Davie Cooper on for the second half, but the gods were not smiling on Rangers that day. Terry Butcher had a goal disallowed and near the end Ally McCoist missed a chance he would normally have taken. So the domestic honours were shared.

Breaking The Mould

As has become usual, summer 1989 was not without its share of news stories from Rangers Football Club. Mel Sterland, after a brief career in a Light Blues shirt, left for Leeds United, and Dave Kirkwood, who had been with Rangers for some years, travelled along the M8 to Hearts. And there were two significant additions to the playing staff.

The English international midfielder Trevor Steven joined his former clubmate Gary Stevens on the Rangers payroll. The fee was later fixed by a tribunal at £1.5 million. But it was the second signing which really set Glasgow buzzing. The man involved was Ally McCoist's regular Scotland striking partner, Maurice Johnston.

Mo's career had taken him to Nantes in France via Celtic and Watford, and indeed his name had been linked again with Celtic. For Rangers to sign him meant breaking the mould in a big way, for Mo was a Catholic and tradition decreed that Catholics went to Celtic and Protestants to Rangers.

That wasn't an edict that Graeme Souness much cared for, as he had made clear from the time he came to Ibrox. He felt it was a problem he shouldn't have to face, and said in an early press interview: "Do the Rangers fans want a successful team or a sectarian one? This is too big a club to be limited to signing only a percentage of the population."

Souness made it clear that he was only

interested in Maurice Johnston as a player, and that the fans should judge him on that basis. The rest we know: Mo has been accepted by the Light Blues faithful and is now an integral part of the team.

The full story of the 1989-90 season is told in another feature in this annual. Rangers took their second Championship in a row, just missed out on another Skol Cup, and can be said to have failed both on the European front and in the Scottish Cup. And, of course, Graeme Souness played his last game for the club.

It is worth taking a wider look at some of the other aspects of Rangers Football Club and the way it is growing, for Graeme Souness is very much involved in these matters. Ibrox Stadium continues to be developed as one of Europe's finest football grounds, with an extra tier on the main stand providing further executive boxes, catering facilities, lounges and meeting rooms.

Graeme Souness and David Murray have a talented team around them to run the club and its many-faceted activities. The early appointment of Walter Smith as assistant manager was crucial, and he has remained a vital part of the team, as have John MacGregor and Phil Boersma on the coaching side. The signing of Davie Dodds made sense too: as well as being an excellent player, Dodds is a qualified SFA coach and will be helping on that side from now on.

The theme continues in other areas. Rangers' match programme and the club newspaper, *Rangers News*, are both recognised as among the best of their kind in Britain. John Greig, whose name is known to Light Blues fans all over the world, has been brought back as public relations executive. It's the same all the way through, and it's all part of a carefully planned long-term programme.

Rangers are, with some flair and originality, capitalising on their name and traditions. The catering has been revitalised with brand-name products including Rangers Crisps as well as a full range of snack foods and, for the executive boxes, top-quality restaurant meals. To go with those meals you can drink Rangers-labelled wines.

As well as all the usual club merchandise such as scarves, posters and so on, you can if you wish complete your ensemble by wearing a kilt in Rangers own tartan. The concept of 'corporate identity' is familiar in business: here it is being applied, top to bottom, to a major football club, and with great success.

Graeme Souness is still only 37: his chairman is one year older. As Graeme looks back on the last four years he can feel that a great deal has been achieved. But he knows also that there is still a lot to be done. The Scottish Cup has not come to Ibrox for a decade and, probably more importantly to him, European success still seems some way off. These are important short to medium-term objectives.

More exciting new faces will arrive: Mark Hateley has joined the strike force for the new season and top Soviet player Oleg Kuznetsov will also appear in the Light Blues strip (how he'll cope with a burst of McCoist patter remains to be seen!). There will be memorable matches, in a stadium fully fitted for them, and there will inevitably be disappointments.

Of one thing we can be sure: while Graeme Souness is in charge, Rangers will continue to make news. It can't be any other way. The flow of 'Rangers Rumours' will continue unabated, but it will be on the pitch that the Rangers manager will want to make most of his points. Souness may not appear as a player again, but in his heart he still thinks of himself as a footballer, and he needs to make the team play for him. He is part of them and they are very much part of him.

The Rangers story, now nearly 120 years long, has never been a boring one. The last decade of this century will certainly not be boring. There are exciting times ahead for Rangers. The story goes on!

Souness The Player

Graeme Souness had a distinguished playing career. Born in Edinburgh, he never played for a Scottish club but went as a teenager to Spurs and then moved to Middlesbrough before signing for Liverpool in 1978 at the age of 25. In the next six years at Anfield, he was a part of an astonishing success story.

During that period Liverpool were League champions five times, League Cup winners four times, and took three European Cups. Souness was appointed club captain by manager Bob Paisley. He was also a regular in the Scotland team, and in all collected 54 caps.

In 1984 Souness moved to Sampdoria, an Italian club based in Genoa. He brought them success also, the club winning the Italian Cup for the first time for many years.

Shortly after joining Rangers as player/manager in April 1986, Graeme Souness went to the Mexico World Cup as captain of Scotland. He was dropped by Alex Ferguson for the last game against Uruguay, but had already decided that

because of the demands of the Rangers job, he would retire from international football.

Souness was fanatical about his fitness. Medical tests before the 1986 World Cup showed him, at the age of 33, to be fully the equal in fitness of any player in the party. As a captain and as a manager, he has demanded the same dedication from the players around him.

Due to injury and the pressure of his other commitments, Graeme Souness made few appearances for Rangers in seasons 1988-89 and 1989-90, and decided to retire as a player at the end of the 89-90 campaign. His last appearance was on Saturday 28 April 1990 as a substitute during the home game with Dunfermline; at the end of the game he received the Championship trophy.

The Souness Honours

1986-87: League champions, Skol Cup winners.

1987-88: Skol Cup winners.

1988-89: League champions, Skol Cup winners, Scottish Cup runners-up.

1989-90: League champions.

Graeme and some of his ̶s̶̶a̶̶n̶̶d̶̶b̶̶a̶̶g̶̶s̶ things model the new outfi

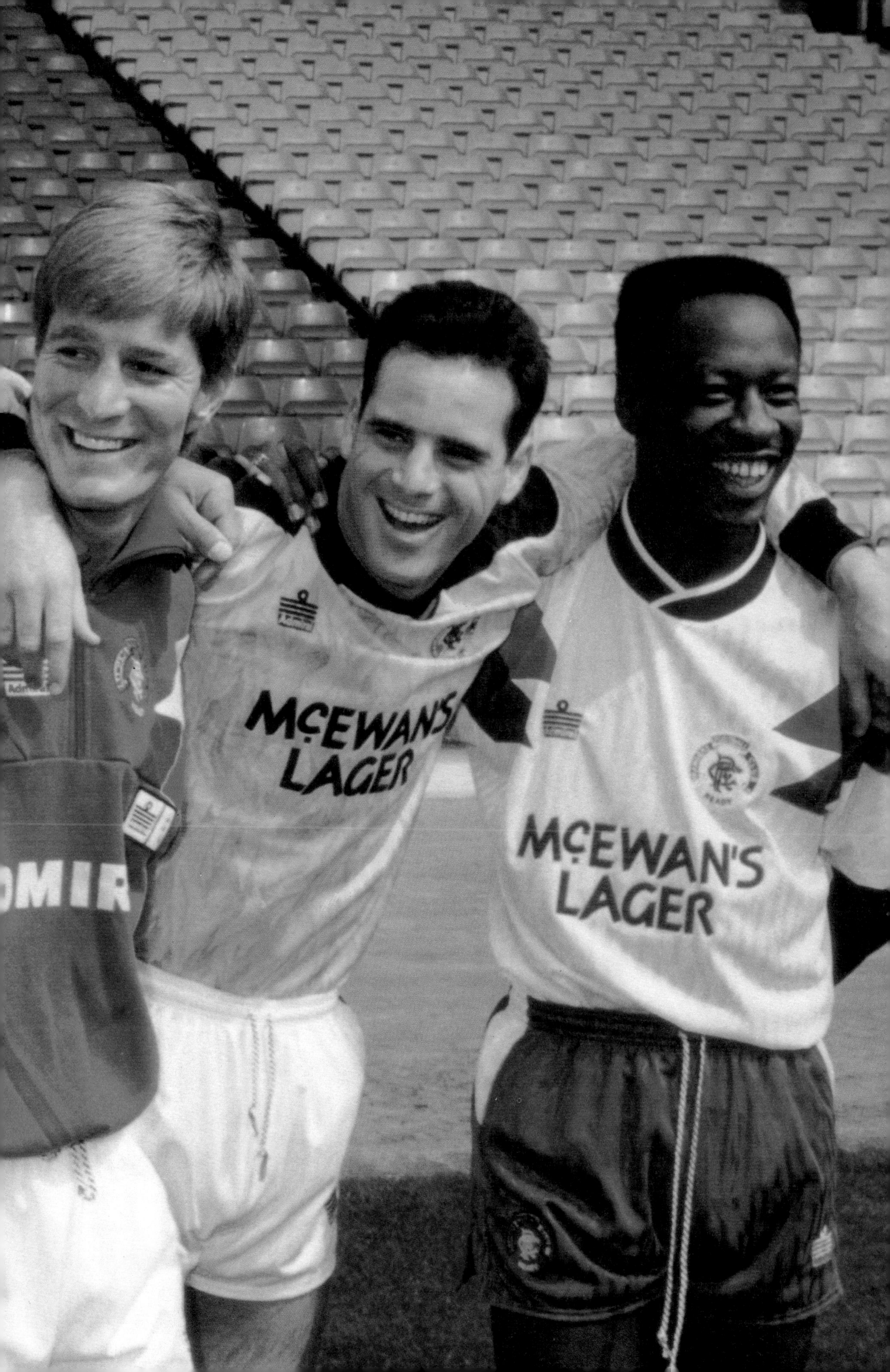
McEWAN'S
LAGER
McEWAN'S
LAGER
OMIR

NIGHT OF TRIUMPH IN BARCELONA

The 1972 Cup-Winners Cup Final

Twenty-seven years after the memorable friendly match with Moscow Dynamo at Ibrox, Rangers faced the Russian side once again. This time there was a great deal at stake for both sides.

For Rangers, it was their third Cup-Winners Cup final. At their first attempt in 1961, they lost out 4-1 on aggregate to Fiorentina in a two-leg match. Six years later there was further disappointment as the trophy went to Bayern Munich by the narrowest of margins, 1-0 after extra time in a game played on German soil at Nuremberg.

Moscow Dynamo too had much to play for: they were the first Soviet side ever to appear in the final of a European competition.

There were no easy ties in the early stages of the competition for Rangers. The first round tie against Rennes of France was won 2-1 on aggregate, an away draw being followed by victory at Ibrox through an Alex MacDonald goal. The second round brought Rangers up against Sporting Lisbon in two extraordinary matches which read more like fiction than fact.

Rangers made a dream start at Ibrox in the first leg. By half-time they were 3-0 ahead with two goals from big Colin Stein and another from Willie Henderson. But the story was by no means over. Lisbon fought back and goals from Chic and Gomes made the final score 3-2 and set up a dramatic return in Lisbon.

In front of 60,000 fans, the Portuguese side attacked from the start and Yazalde tied the scores in the 26th minute. Back came Rangers and within two minutes Colin Stein had restored their lead. Tome scored again for the Lisbon side to make the half-time score 2-1, and 4-4 on aggregate.

Rangers came out for the second half like a team inspired, and Stein restored the overall lead immediately on the restart. For half an hour Rangers defended their lead resolutely, but Sporting's pressure was intense and with just seven minutes to go Gomes scored to make it 5-5 and force extra time.

There were two goals during the extra period — Willie Henderson netting for the Light Blues and Perez for Lisbon. With the score at the end of an exhausting two hours of football 4-3 on the night and 6-6 on aggregate, Rangers thought they had won by scoring more away goals. But the referee had other ideas, and ordered a penalty shoot-out to decide the tie.

Sporting won the shoot-out, and a dejected Rangers team went back to their dressing-room thinking they were out of the cup. But the drama was not yet over. A UEFA rulebook was produced and studied, and it was found that, astonishingly, the referee was wrong. The penalty shoot-out was invalid — Rangers had won!

After all that, the third round against Torino was almost an anti-climax, Rangers winning through with another Alex MacDonald special for a 2-1 aggregate. The semi-final draw could hardly have been tougher: the mighty Bayern Munich stood between Rangers and the final, with the first leg away from home.

A battling performance by a side superbly marshalled by John Greig saw Rangers cancel out Breitner's 24th minute strike with an equaliser after 49 minutes, when Colin Stein's shot was put into his own net by Zobel as he desperately tried to clear.

The return at Ibrox, with 80,000 fans packed into the ground, held high drama right from the start. In the first minute Sandy Jardine crashed in a shot which goalkeeper Sepp Maier could only watch as it flew into the net. Inspired Rangers pressed forward and Derek Parlane, playing in his first European tie as replacement for the injured John Greig, scored the second to book the Light Blues their place in the final.

Drama In Spain

So the stage was set, and Rangers travelled to Barcelona determined to give everything to bring the cup back to Ibrox. They could not have wished for better support — of the crowd of 35,000 some 20,000 were Rangers fans who had travelled to Spain by any means possible. In contrast, Dynamo had just 400 supporters with them.

In the early stages, play swung from end to end as the teams strove for supremacy. McCloy had to make a good stop from midfielder Dolbonosov; Tommy McLean replied with a great shot from 25 yards which brought a full-length save from Pilgui.

In the 24th minute came the moment the Light Blues fans had been waiting for. Johnston crossed from the right and Colin Stein netted from eight yards to give Rangers the lead.

The goal was unfortunately followed by the first of several incidents as Rangers fans invaded the pitch. Play was held up for several minutes, but it was Dynamo who seemed the more rattled, and six minutes before half-time a cross from Dave Smith, the outstanding player on the park, was headed home by Willie Johnston.

Four minutes into the second half, the cup seemed destined for Ibrox. A typical long McCloy kick-out was moved on by Stein to Johnston, who put away his second goal of the night to give Rangers a 3-0 advantage.

But the Russians were not done with yet. On came Eschtrekov as a substitute for Jakobik, and on the hour he gave Dynamo hope, beating McCloy to reduce the deficit to 3-1. The Moscow team threw everything at Rangers, and the Light Blues defence performed heroics, inspired by Greig and with McCloy having a fine game in goal.

Smith made a goal-line stop and an attempted clearance from Sandy Jardine sliced narrowly past his own post. Three minutes from time, the relentless Dynamo pressure told when Mahovikov pulled another one back.

Those three minutes seemed like thirty to the team and their supporters, but Rangers held out. After 16 years and 83 European matches, Rangers had won the Cup-Winners Cup!

Unable to contain their joy, fans poured onto the pitch in their thousands, disrupting proceedings so much that John Greig had to receive the massive trophy in the dressing-room. Dynamo lodged a protest with UEFA, claiming that the match had finished early. After an inquiry, the result stood, but Rangers were unable to defend the cup the following season — as a result of the pitch invasions they were banned from European competition for two years (later reduced to one year on appeal).

But nothing could spoil the joy of that moment of triumph in Barcelona. It was almost Willie Waddell's last act as manager. Within two weeks he had become general manager of the club, with Jock Wallace taking over in charge of the team.

Teams: *Rangers*: Peter McCloy, Sandy Jardine, Willie Mathieson, John Greig, Derek Johnstone, Dave Smith, Tommy McLean, Alfie Conn, Colin Stein, Alex MacDonald, Willie Johnston.
Moscow Dynamo: Pilgui, Basalaycev, Dolmatov, Zykov, Dolbonosov (Gerschkovich), Zukov, Baidazhnyi, Jakobik (Eschtrekov), Sabo, Mahovikov, Evriuschkin.

Celebrations

Aftermath

Colin Stein scores Rangers' opening goal

PRIZE QUIZ

TEST your knowledge and WIN a FABULOUS DAY at IBROX. Full V.I.P. treatment for two on a Match Day (to be arranged with lucky Winners). The Prize includes Lunch, Match Tickets and other *"extras"* — in short, a never-to-be-forgotten day out for any Rangers fan!

Rangers in Europe

1. Name the first Rangers player to be sent off in a European competition.

2. An Italian team were the first victors at Ibrox in any European competition. Which team?

3. Rangers defeated Dynamo Kiev 2-0 in the first round (second leg) of the European Cup at Ibrox season 1987/88. Who scored for Rangers?

4. The same two players both scored in the next round home tie v. Gornik. Who scored Rangers' other goal in the 3-1 victory?

5. Rangers' record win in Europe was 10-1 v. Valetta of Malta. True or False?

6. Name the team who scored an aggregate **eight** goals against Rangers in the 1962-63 Cup Winners' Cup.

7. Season 1988/89 Katowice of Poland lost 1-0 at Ibrox in the UEFA Cup. What was the score in the return game in Poland?

8. Jim Bett scored only one European goal for Rangers. Against which team?

9. What happened to centre-half Ron McKinnon in Portugal during the 1971-72 Cup Winners' Cup match v. Sporting Lisbon?

10. Who defeated Rangers in the first round of the 1976/77 season European Cup?

Fun Quiz Answers

Rangers in the Skol and Scottish Cups

1. Derek Ferguson.
2. Ally McCoist and Paul Mason (Aberdeen) shared with **five** goals each.
3. Ian Durrant, Davie Cooper and Robert Fleck.
4. Ally McCoist.
5. 2-1 against Celtic. Ian Durrant and Davie Cooper (penalty) scored.
6. Dundee.
7. Ally Dawson.
8. Celtic. Rangers won 3-2.
9. Hamilton.
10. Aberdeen.

Rangers' League Campaigns

1. Kevin Drinkell.
2. He scored Rangers' first ever Premier League goal in the 2-1 victory over Celtic.
3. Hearts.
4. True . . . and the League Cup and the Scottish Cup!
5. Celtic (in the first minute!). Celtic won 2-1.
6. Morton. Mark Falco (3), Ally McCoist (3) and Robert Fleck.
7. Jimmy Duncanson.
8. Ian Durrant.
9. Aberdeen at Ibrox.
10. Terry Butcher, Ian Ferguson and Mark Walters (2).

Pick of the Season
RANGERS *v Celtic*
Rangers 3 — Celtic 0, 1st April 1990

encourages Ally before the second penalty

Goal no. 2

Terry can't bear to watch the Walters pena...

THE ultimate hurdle for Rangers on this *'day of fools'* — Celtic at Ibrox.

Celtic, riding high after their Scottish Cup defeat of the Light Blues five weeks earlier.

Rangers were stuttering towards a second consecutive title after having established a commanding lead at the top of the Premier League. A poor six-week spell had realised only draws against Dundee, St Mirren, Motherwell and Hearts and a home defeat by Hibernian the week prior to Celtic's visit.

Celtic began confidently enough, yet Rangers drew first blood. Midway through the first half, Richard Gough rose with Anton Rogan to meet Terry Butcher's hoisted cross into the Celtic box.

Inexplicably Rogan handled. Maybe he was waving to a friend in the crowd, maybe it was an elaborate April Fool's Day joke. But penalty it certainly was.

Mark Walters stepped forward to hit a low right foot shot which, although Pat Bonner got a hand to, nested surely in the Celtic net. The rejoicing began.

Goal No. 2 was a beauty! Richard Gough was again involved as he won the ball for Ally McCoist in a crunching tackle on Paul McStay. Ally advanced before releasing a perfect pass to Mo Johnston, who had created space outside the box.

His sweet half volley, after chesting the ball down as Paul Elliot closed in, was a joy to

behold. Bonner was left helpless and Rangers were two up. The *Champions Elect* were looking the part.

Penalty hero Mark Walters was also involved in goal No. 3 as, faced by Derek Whyte, he crossed high into the Celtic area. Mo Johnston was fouled by Peter Grant. Spot kick No. 2!

Ally McCoist was about to take his rightful place in the history books. In scoring, he would break the Ibrox postwar record of league goals jointly held with Derek Johnstone. Destiny was his. Rangers were three goals ahead and cruising to victory.

Celtic greeted the final whistle with some relief.

Certainly it was still possible for Rangers **NOT** to win the championship but in the end, their timing was perfect. Perhaps it had been planned that way.

JOHN GREIG

John Greig is a Rangers man through and through, his connection with Ibrox going back 30 years to the time when he signed as a youngster in August 1960. Before that John, an Edinburgh lad, confesses to having been a Hearts supporter!

Within two years, John Greig was challenging for a first-team place, and made his European debut in the 1961-62 season along with another 18-year-old, Willie Henderson. By 1963 Greig was a regular in the Rangers midfield and in that year he collected the first of his five Championship medals.

By 1966 John Greig was captain of Rangers and was named as Scottish Player of the Year, an award he lifted again a decade later. He took the team to Scottish Cup triumphs in 1966, 1973 and 1976, having already played in winning sides in 1962 and 1963.

His qualities of leadership as well as his considerable talents as a player led to 44 caps for Scotland, and he wore the dark blue jersey with great distinction with appearances in the World Cup finals in 1974.

It was not, of course, all success. Greig was club captain throughout the period from 1966 to 1974 when Celtic won nine Championships in a row, Rangers finishing second six times behind the Parkhead club. In April 1975 that was all put right when Rangers drew with Hibernian at Easter Road to take the Championship back to Ibrox. John Greig was injured and unable to make a full appearance, but to the great delight of the fans he came on for the last few minutes to take a deserved share of the glory. John also had to suffer the notorious match in January 1967 when Berwick Rangers knocked the Light Blues out of the Scottish Cup at the first hurdle; and he was captain at the time of the tragic happenings of 2 January 1971, when 66 people died at Ibrox after steel barriers on a stair gave way.

But the happier memories are those which live on. One of the happiest was in May 1972 when John led Rangers to glory in the European Cup-Winners Cup, taking the trophy in a dramatic match in which Moscow Dynamo were defeated 3-2.

In May 1978 John Greig was unexpectedly moved from dressing-room to manager's chair when Jock Wallace resigned. His playing career ended after 857 senior appearances for the Light Blues: had he not been promoted to manager he would almost certainly have broken Dougie Gray's record of 879 games for the club.

During John Greig's six years as manager, Rangers had only limited success, failing to win the Premier League. In cup competitions they fared better, taking the Scottish Cup twice, in 1979 and 1981, being beaten finalists in 1980, 1982 and 1983, and collecting the League Cup three times.

John Greig resigned as manager in October 1984 but maintained the connection with the club he had served so well and in the 1989-90 season was given the job of looking after the public relations side at Ibrox, a task for which, with his experience and enthusiasm, he is ideally suited.

The press nicknamed John Greig 'Mr Rangers' during his playing and managerial career, and his outstanding service to Scottish football was recognised by the award of the MBE in 1977.

ITALIA '90
Mixed Fortunes for Rangers Stars

Scotland v. Poland friendly before the finals

Seven Rangers players travelled to the World Cup finals in Italy. Mo Johnston, Richard Gough and Ally McCoist were in the Scotland squad: Terry Butcher, Trevor Steven, Gary Stevens and Chris Woods were with England. To say that they enjoyed mixed fortunes is something of an understatement.

The three Scots all saw action, but for Richard Gough there was great disappointment when he had to return home early through injury — and it was a blow for Scotland too. Mo Johnston scored in the fine win over Sweden, a clean strike from the penalty spot after he had been fouled, but the tournament ended for the Scots at the first stage.

England, of course, made it through to the semi-finals, Butcher in particular playing a major part. Trevor Steven and Gary Stevens were involved at the later stages and Trevor impressed both when coming on as a substitute defender and with his midfield play in England's last two matches.

Chris Woods was on the bench for every England match but was not called into action, England manager Bobby Robson sticking with

Peter Shilton, who was indeed one of the best keepers in the whole competition. Shilton has now announced his retirement from international football, so hopefully Chris will be England's no 1 in the season ahead.

Results

Scotland (First Stage Only)
Scotland 0, Costa Rica 1
Scotland 2, Sweden 1
Scotland 0, Brazil 1

England — First Stage
England 1, Ireland 1
England 0, Holland 0
England 1, Egypt 0

Second Stage
England 1, Belgium 0 (after extra time)

Quarter-Final
England 3, Cameroon 2 (after extra time)

Semi-Final
England 1, West Germany 1 (W. Germany won penalty shoot-out)

The Rangers Shop

SOMETIMES IT'S TOUGH AT THE TOP...

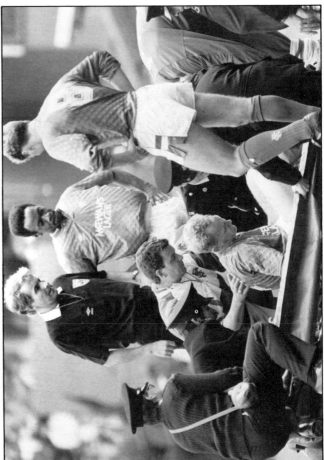

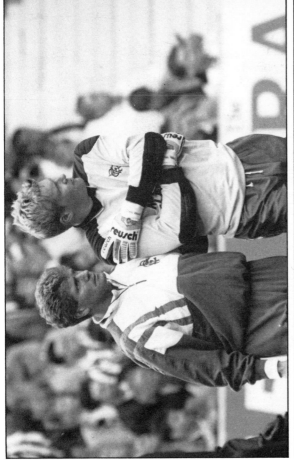

FIRST-TEAM STATISTICS

DATE	OPPONENTS		COMP.	SCORE	ATT.	G	2	3	
Aug.12	ST MIRREN	(H)	L	0-1	39,951	Woods	Stevens	Munro	C
Aug. 15	ARBROATH	(H)	SK	4-0	31,726	Ginzburg	Stevens	Munro	G
Aug. 19	HIBERNIAN	(A)	L	0-2	22,000	Ginzburg	Stevens	Munro	G
Aug. 22	MORTON	(A)	SK	2-1	8,000	Ginzburg	Stevens	Munro	N
Aug. 26	CELTIC	(A)	L	1-1	54,000	Ginzburg	Stevens	Munro	G
Aug. 29	HAMILTON	(A)	SK	3-0	9,162	Ginzburg	Stevens	Munro	B
Sept. 9	ABERDEEN	(H)	L	1-0	40,283	Woods	Stevens	Munro	B
Sept. 13	BAYERN MUN.	(H)	EC	1-3	40,153	Woods	Stevens	Munro	N
Sept. 16	DUNDEE	(H)	L	2-2	35,836	Woods	Stevens	Munro	N
Sept. 19	DUNFERMLINE	(A)	SK	5-0	41,648	Woods	Stevens	Munro	G
Sept. 23	DUNFERMLINE	(A)	L	1-1	17,765	Woods	Stevens	Munro	G
Sept. 27	BAYERN MUN.	(A)	EC	0-0	40,000	Ginzburg	Stevens	Munro	G
Sept. 30	HEARTS	(H)	L	1-0	39,544	Ginzburg	Stevens	Munro	G
Oct. 3	MOTHERWELL	(A)	L	0-1	17,667	Ginzburg	Stevens	Munro	G
Oct. 14	DUNDEE UTD	(H)	L	2-1	36,062	Woods	Stevens	Munro	G
Oct. 22	ABERDEEN	(HP)	SK	1-2	61,190	Woods	Stevens	Munro	G
Oct. 25	ST MIRREN	(A)	L	2-0	13,247	Woods	Stevens	Munro	G
Oct. 28	HIBERNIAN	(H)	L	3-0	35,260	Woods	Stevens	Munro	G
Nov. 4	CELTIC	(H)	L	1-0	41,598	Woods	Stevens	Munro	B
Nov. 18	DUNDEE	(A)	L	2-0	14,536	Woods	Stevens	Munro	B
Nov. 22	ABERDEEN	(A)	L	0-1	22,500	Woods	Stevens	Munro	B
Nov. 25	DUNFERMLINE	(H)	L	3-0	39,131	Woods	Stevens	Munro	B
Dec. 2	HEARTS	(A)	L	2-1	24,771	Woods	Stevens	Munro	B
Dec. 9	MOTHERWELL	(H)	L	3-0	33,549	Woods	Stevens	Munro	G
Dec. 16	DUNDEE UTD	(A)	L	1-1	15,947	Woods	Stevens	Munro	G
Dec. 19	ARSENAL	(H)	ZC	1-2	31,118	Woods	Stevens	Munro	G
Dec. 23	ST MIRREN	(H)	L	1-0	31,797	Woods	Stevens	Munro	G
Dec. 30	HIBERNIAN	(A)	L	0-0	22,000	Woods	Stevens	Munro	G
Jan. 2	CELTIC	(A)	L	1-0	54,000	Woods	Stevens	Munro	G
Jan. 6	ABERDEEN	(H)	L	2-0	41,351	Woods	Stevens	Munro	G
Jan. 13	DUNDEE	(H)	L	3-0	36,993	Woods	Stevens	Munro	G
Jan. 20	ST JOHNSTONE	(H)	SC	3-0	39,003	Woods	Stevens	Munro	G
Jan. 27	DUNFERMLINE	(A)	L	1-0	17,350	Woods	**Stevens**	Munro	G
Feb. 3	DUNDEE UTD	(H)	L	3-1	39,058	Woods	Stevens	Munro	G
Feb. 10	MOTHERWELL	(A)	L	1-1	17,647	Woods	Stevens	Munro	I. Fe
Feb. 17	HEARTS	(H)	L	0-0	41,884	Woods	Stevens	Munro	I. Fe
Feb. 25	CELTIC	(A)	SC	0-1	52,565	Woods	Stevens	Munro	I. Fe
Mar. 3	DUNDEE	(A)	L	2-2	13,500	Woods	Stevens	Munro	N
Mar. 17	ST MIRREN	(A)	L	0-0	16,129	Woods	Stevens	Munro	G
Mar. 24	HIBERNIAN	(H)	L	0-1	37,542	Woods	Stevens	Munro	G
Apr. 1	CELTIC	(H)	L	3-0	41,926	Woods	Stevens	Munro	G
Apr. 8	ABERDEEN	(A)	L	0-0	22,000	Woods	Stevens	Munro	G
Apr. 14	MOTHERWELL	(H)	L	2-1	39,305	Woods	Brown	Munro	G
Apr. 21	DUNDEE UTD	(A)	L	1-0	15,995	Woods	Stevens	Munro	G
Apr. 28	DUNFERMLINE	(H)	L	2-0	40,769	Woods	Stevens	Munro	G
May 5	HEARTS	(A)	L	1-1	20,283	Woods	Stevens	**Munro**	G

• SCORERS ARE IN BOLD TYPE • KEY: L — LEAGUE; SC — SCOTTISH CUP; SK — SKOL CUP; EC — EUROPEAN CU

RANGERS FOOTBALL CLUB

CHAIRMAN

David Murray

VICE-CHAIRMAN

Jack Gillespie

DIRECTORS

David Murray, Jack Gillespie,

Graeme Souness

Campbell Ogilvie, Hugh Adam

HONORARY DIRECTOR

W. T. O. Waddell

SECRETARY

Campbell Ogilvie

Player	Premier			Skol			Euro			
	A	S	G	A	S	G	A	S	G	A
JOHNSTON	36	—	15	5	—	1	2	—	—	2
MUNRO	36	—	1	5	—	2	2	—	—	2
STEVENS	35	—	1	5	—	—	2	—	—	2
STEVEN	34	—	3	5	—	2	2	—	—	2
BUTCHER	34	—	3	5	—	—	2	—	—	2
McCOIST	31	1	14	4	—	5	—	—	—	2
WOODS	32	—	—	2	—	—	1	—	—	2
WALTERS	27	—	5	5	—	3	2	—	1	2
GOUGH	26	—	—	4	—	—	1	—	—	1
BROWN	24	3	1	1	—	—	—	—	—	2
I. FERGUSON	20	3	—	4	1	2	2	—	—	1
WILKINS	15	—	—	5	—	—	2	—	—	
SPACKMAN	21	—	1	—	—	—	—	—	—	2
GINZBURG	4	—	—	3	—	—	1	—	—	
D. FERGUSON	4	1	—	1	—	—	1	—	—	
NISBET	4	3	—	1	—	—	1	—	—	
DRINKELL	2	2	—	1	1	—	1	—	1	—
McCALL	2	2	—	—	1	—	—	—	—	
COWAN	1	2	—	—	—	—	1	—	—	
COOPER	1	1	—	—	—	—	—	—	—	
DODDS	3	10	4	—	—	—	—	—	—	
VINNICOMBE	1	5	—	—	—	—	—	—	—	
ROBERTSON	—	1	—	—	—	—	—	—	—	
SOUNESS	—	1	—	—	—	—	—	—	—	

• KEY: A — APPEARANCES; S — SUBSTITUTE; G — GOALS SCORED

	6	7	8	9	10	11	12	14
s	Butcher	Steven	D. Ferguson	McCoist	Johnston	Walters	I. Ferguson	Drinkell
s	Butcher	Steven	**I. Ferguson**	**McCoist 3**	Johnston	Walters	D. Ferguson	Drinkell
s	Butcher	Steven	I. Ferguson	McCoist	Johnston	Walters	Nisbet	Drinkell
s	**Butcher**	Steven	I. Ferguson	Drinkell	Johnston	Brown	McCoist	Brown
s	Butcher	**Steven**	I. Ferguson	McCoist	Johnston	**Walters 2**	Nisbet	Drinkell
s	Butcher	Steven	I. Ferguson	Drinkell	**Johnston**	Walters	Nisbet	McCoist
s	Butcher	Steven	I. Ferguson	D. Ferguson	Johnston	**Walters**	Not Used	Not Used
s	Butcher	Steven	D. Ferguson	**McCoist 2**	Johnston	Walters	Drinkell	I. Ferguson
s	Butcher	**Steven**	D. Ferguson	**McCoist 2**	**Johnston**	Walters	**I. Ferguson**	Drinkell
s	Butcher	Steven	D. Ferguson	**McCoist**	Johnston	Walters	I. Ferguson	Drinkell
s	Butcher	Steven	I. Ferguson	Cowan	Johnston	Walters	Drinkell	Not Used
s	Butcher	Steven	I. Ferguson	McCoist	**Johnston**	Walters	Cowan	Dodds
s	Butcher	Steven	Dodds	McCoist	Johnston	Cooper	McCall	Cowan
s	Butcher	Steven	Cooper	**McCoist**	**Johnston**	Walters	McCall	Dodds
s	Butcher	Steven	I. Ferguson	McCoist	Johnston	**Walters**	McCall	Brown
s	Butcher	Steven	I. Ferguson	**McCoist**	**Johnston**	McCall	Dodds	Cowan
s	Butcher	Steven	I. Ferguson	**McCoist 2**	**Johnston**	McCall	Dodds	Cowan
s	Butcher	Steven	I. Ferguson	McCoist	**Johnston**	Walters	Dodds	Nisbet
s	Butcher	Steven	I. Ferguson	McCoist	**Johnston**	**Walters**	Dodds	Nisbet
s	Butcher	Steven	I. Ferguson	McCoist	Johnston	Walters	Dodds	Nisbet
s	**Butcher**	Steven	I. Ferguson	**McCoist**	**Johnston**	Walters	Dodds	Nisbet
nan	Butcher	**Steven**	I. Ferguson	McCoist	Johnston	**Walters**	Dodds	Cowan
nan	**Butcher**	Steven	I. Ferguson	**McCoist**	Johnston	**Brown**	Dodds	Vinnicombe
nan	Butcher	Steven	I. Ferguson	McCoist	**Johnston**	Brown	Dodds	Vinnicombe
nan	Butcher	Steven	I. Ferguson	Walters	**Johnston**	Brown	Ginzburg	Cowan
nan	Butcher	Steven	I. Ferguson	McCoist	Johnston	Brown	**Dodds**	Vinnicombe
nan	Butcher	Walters	Cowan	McCoist	Johnston	Brown	Dodds	Vinnicombe
nan	Butcher	Steven	Walters	McCoist	Johnston	Brown	Dodds	Vinnicombe
nan	Butcher	Steven	**Walters**	**McCoist**	Johnston	Brown	Dodds	Vinnicombe
nan	Butcher	Steven	Walters	**McCoist**	**Johnston**	Brown	**Dodds**	Vinnicombe
nan	Butcher	Steven	**Walters**	McCoist	**Johnston**	**Brown**	Dodds	Vinnicombe
nan	Nisbet	Steven	Walters	McCoist	Johnston	Brown	Dodds	Vinnicombe
nan	Vinnicombe	Steven	**Walters**	**McCoist**	**Johnston**	Brown	Dodds	Robertson
nan	Butcher	Steven	Walters	McCoist	**Johnston**	Brown	Dodds	Vinnicombe
nan	Butcher	Steven	Walters	McCoist	Johnston	Brown	Dodds	Vinnicombe
nan	Butcher	Steven	Walters	McCoist	Johnston	Brown	Dodds	Vinnicombe
nan	Butcher	Steven	I. Ferguson	**Dodds**	**Johnston**	Brown	Vinnicombe	Robertson
nan	Butcher	Steven	I. Ferguson	Nisbet	Johnston	Brown	Dodds	Vinnicombe
nan	Butcher	Steven	Walters	McCoist	Johnston	Brown	I. Ferguson	Dodds
nan	Butcher	Steven	I. Ferguson	**McCoist**	**Johnston**	**Walters**	Brown	Dodds
nan	Butcher	Steven	I. Ferguson	McCoist	Johnston	Walters	Brown	Dodds
nan	Butcher	**Steven**	Dodds	McCoist	**Johnston**	Walters	Nisbet	D. Ferguson
nan	Butcher	**Steven**	D. Ferguson	McCoist	Johnston	Walters	Brown	Dodds
nan	Butcher	Steven	Brown	**McCoist**	Johnston	Walters	Souness	**Dodds**
nan	Butcher	Dodds	Brown	McCoist	Johnston	Walters	Cooper	Vinnicombe

ZENITH CHALLENGE; HP — HAMPDEN PARK

PREMIER DIVISION CHAMPIONSHIP
(FINAL PLACINGS SEASON 1989/90)

	P	W	D	L	F	A	Pt
Rangers	36	20	11	5	48	19	51
Aberdeen	36	17	10	9	56	33	44
Heart of Midlothian .	36	16	12	8	54	35	44
Dundee United	36	11	14	11	36	39	35
Celtic	36	10	14	12	37	37	34
Motherwell	36	11	12	13	43	47	34
Hibs	36	12	10	14	34	41	34
Dunfermline	36	11	8	17	37	50	30
St Mirren	36	10	10	16	28	48	30
Dundee	36	5	14	17	41	65	24

DIRECTORY
RANGERS FOOTBALL CLUB plc
Ibrox Stadium, 150 Edmiston Drive, Glasgow G51 2XD

Ticket Office 041-427 8800
Season Tickets &
Supporters Club Enquiries 041-427 8811
Commercial and Marketing 041-427 8822
Restaurant, Conference & Banqueting ...041-427 8833
Rangers News & Programmes 041-427 8844
Rangers Hotline 0898 121 555
Administration 041-427 8500
Fax Number 041-427 2676
Edmiston Club, 100 Edmiston Drive 041-427 4481
Rangers Pools Ltd., 11 Harrison Drive ...041-427 4914
Rangers Supporters Association,
250 Edmiston Drive, Social Club 041-427 2902
General Secretary 041-427 4593

G
17
1
1
5
3
19
—
10
—
2
2
—
1
—
—
1
—
—
4
—
—

CLUB HONOURS

EUROPEAN CUP WINNERS CUP

Winners 1972

Runners up 1961, 1967

LEAGUE CHAMPIONS: (40)

1891*1899 1900 1901 1902 1911 1912 1913 1918
1920 1921 1923 1924 1925 1927 1928 1929 1930
1931 1933 1934 1935 1937 1939 1947 1949 1950
1953 1956 1957 1959 1961 1963 1964 1975 1976
1978 1987 1989 1990

*In 1891, the Championship was shared with Dumbarton.

SCOTTISH CUP WINNERS: (24)

1894 1897 1898 1903 1928 1930 1932 1934 1935
1936 1948 1949 1950 1953 1960 1962 1963 1964
1966 1973 1976 1978 1979 1981.

LEAGUE CUP WINNERS: (16)

1946/47, 1948/49, 1960/61, 1961/62, 1963/64,
1964/65, 1970/71, 1975/76, 1977/78, 1978/79,
1981/82, 1983/84, 1984/85, 1986/87, 1987/88,
1988/89.

ACKNOWLEDGEMENTS

Published by Holmes McDougall Limited, Allander House, 137-141 Leith Walk, Edinburgh EH6 8NS, Scotland.

Printed and bound in Scotland.
Design & Artwork by David C. Wilson.
Written by Roger Smith.
Match reports on pages 2, 27 and 53 by Douglas Russell.

All photographs supplied by *The Evening Times* except Page 28, supplied by *The Glaswegian*.
Edited by John Traynor and Douglas Russell (Holmes McDougall Limited).

Every effort has been made by the publishers to ensure the accuracy of all details and information in this publication.

WILD THINGS!

Tiger
at the door

Lisa Regan

ILLUSTRATED BY **Kelly Caswell**

BLOOMSBURY

LONDON NEW DELHI NEW YORK SYDNEY

Published 2013 by
Bloomsbury Publishing Plc
50 Bedford Square, London, WC1B 3DP

www.bloomsbury.com

ISBN   HB 978-1-4081-7935-2
       PB 978-1-4081-7936-9

Produced for Bloomsbury Publishing by Calcium. www.calciumcreative.co.uk

Illustrated by Kelly Caswell

Picture acknowledgements: Shutterstock: Ammit 23tl, Pat138241 23tr.

Printed in China by Toppan Leefung

HB 10 9 8 7 6 5 4 3 2 1
PB 10 9 8 7 6 5 4 3 2 1

FSC
www.fsc.org
MIX
Paper from
responsible sources
FSC® C104723

Contents

Ring, ring. Wild thing!

If you're WILD about animals, today's your lucky day.

There's a tiger at the door! Are you brave enough to invite it in?

Watch out!

This scary visitor wants to look around.

5

Chomp!

The teeth of a tiger are absolutely huge.

Each front tooth is longer than your finger.

Don't get too close!

6

'Aaah'

You will need

A very large toothbrush

A very brave dentist

7

Lick!

A tiger's tongue is really rough.

You will need

A suit of armour

It is covered in bumps that scrape meat off the bones of **prey**.

Don't let your tiger lick you!

Ouch!

9

Hidden

Tigers are silent when they move. They are also well **camouflaged.**

Tigers creep up on other animals without being seen or heard.

You will need

To keep an eye on your tiger - all of the time

Boo!

Never play hide and
seek with your tiger.

11

Feed me!

Tigers are the biggest of all cats.

That means they need to eat a lot of meat.

You will need

Deer

Pigs

Cattle

Buffalo

And a very big garden to keep them all in!

Menu

These hungry giants can eat a large animal every week.

Mmm!

13

Rotten

A tiger never ever wastes its food.

It hides it from other animals and eats it later, even if it has gone bad!

You will need

Air freshener

Disinfectant

Pond cleaner

Sometimes tigers even hide food underwater to keep it safe.

Yuck!

15

Scratch!

Tigers scrape their claws on everything around them.

This keeps the claws super sharp.

You will need

New furniture

Tigers mark objects with their claws to tell other tigers to stay away!

Clear off!

17

Time to go home

Your tiger seems happy, but your parents aren't!

It's time to post your pet back to its real home...

A goldfish makes a great pet, but a tiger is a WILD THING!

19

Cool creatures

Tigers live in 13 countries, including Russia, China, and **Indonesia**.

Unlike many cat **species**, tigers love water and are very good swimmers.

The biggest tigers are larger than any other wild cats. They reach over 2 metres long and have a metre-long tail.

In the dark, a tiger's sight is six times more powerful than a person's.

A tiger's claws grow up to 10 centimetres long.

Male tigers can weigh over 200 kilograms – that's more than a baby elephant!

Glossary

buffalo a large cow-like animal

camouflaged coloured to blend in with the natural surroundings

disinfectant a liquid that kills germs and gets rid of bad smells

Indonesia a group of countries in Asia

prey an animal that is hunted and eaten by other animals

species a type of animal

suit of armour a 'suit' of metal that protects the body

22

Thanks for having me!

The Zoological Society of London (ZSL) is a charity that provides help for animals at home and worldwide. We also run ZSL London Zoo and ZSL Whipsnade Zoo.

By buying this book, you have helped us raise money to continue our work with animals around the world.

Find out more at zsl.org

ZSL
LIVING CONSERVATION

ZSL LONDON ZOO

ZSL WHIPSNADE ZOO

Take them all home!

ISBN   HB 978-1-4081-7937-6
        PB 978-1-4081-7938-3

ISBN   HB 978-1-4081-4247-9
        PB 978-1-4081-5678-0

ISBN   HB 978-1-4081-4246-2
        PB 978-1-4081-5679-7

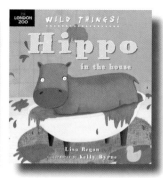

ISBN   HB 978-1-4081-4245-5
        PB 978-1-4081-5680-3

ISBN   HB 978-1-4081-4244-8
        PB 978-1-4081-5681-0

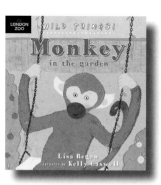

ISBN   HB 978-1-4081-7939-0
        PB 978-1-4081-7940-6

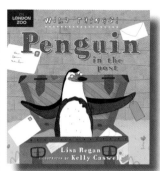

ISBN   HB 978-1-4081-7941-3
        PB 978-1-4081-7942-0

ISBN   HB 978-1-4081-7935-2
        PB 978-1-4081-7936-9